BARRON'S

STUDENT SUCCESS SECRETS

by Eric Jensen

Illustrations by
Charles McPherson

Third Edition

Barron's Educational Series, Inc.
New York • London • Toronto • Sydney

"There are no limitations to the self. There are no limitations to its potential. You can adopt artificial limitations through ignorance."

Jane Roberts

All inquiries should be addressed to:
Barron's Educational Series, Inc.
250 Wireless Boulevard
Hauppauge, New York 11788

International Standard Book No. 0-8120-4233-6

Jensen, Eric.
    Student success secrets / by Eric Jensen: illustrations by
Charles McPherson.—3rd ed.
        p.   cm.
     Bibliography: p.
     ISBN 0-8120-4233-6
     1. Study, Method of. 2. Report writing. 3. Reading comprehension. 4. Note-taking. I. Title.
LB1049.J43 1989
371.3'028'1—dc20   89-6603
                                                          CIP

PRINTED IN THE UNITED STATES OF AMERICA
901   800   98765432

CONTENTS

FIGURES

TABLES

PREFACE

This book had its beginnings several years ago. I realized that there were many study guides available to students, but none had become a classic. I believe that previous "how to study" books presented information but did not give the tools and motivation necessary to implement information.

This book is different. It will provide you with much more than just information. This book will provide you with simple, effective, and dynamic tools to become a superior student. It will motivate you to use these tools each and every day, as you must do to succeed.

I began this book by compiling data from years of teaching in a highly progressive private school. I used the techniques included in this book with over 10,000 students. I inspired them to dramatic heights in the achievement of learning skills. In addition, I researched countless books in order to simplify the path to becoming a successful student.

This book is based on my research and experience. It conveys the enthusiasm and attitude that has been proven successful time and again. This book has everything you need to become a successful student. I have enjoyed writing it and I know you will enjoy reading it. Because you chose to read this book, I know you are ready for the success you deserve. Congratulations and happy reading!

INTRODUCTION

Everybody likes to be successful. Yet, success is not getting A's in school, being popular, getting a scholarship, or making money. Success is a gut-level feeling of confidence and achievement. It is a powerful state of mind wherein the world is yours for the asking. It is a joyous world of unlimited opportunity and choices.

The unhappiest person is the person without choices. To acquire more choices, you need assets. The personal assets you have increase your opportunities and choices in life. Education can be a definite asset, whether formal or informal. It can open up many doors that were previously closed, so get the best education you can. Even if you don't use the academic information, you may use the contacts you make in school later on in life.

This means that you should go to the best school you can afford. It may help you get a better education and have an opportunity to associate with more successful students and staff. In addition, your school's reputation will be carried with you for years.

Once you have chosen your place of education, do the very best you can. Success is an important habit to establish—good habits formed in school will be with you all your life. The whole purpose of this book is to help give you the tools to form those success habits. I applaud your decision to read and use this book. A better tool could not have been chosen!

DAILY SCROLL

Today, this new day, I am a successful student. Overnight my mind and body have produced thousands of new cells to give me the greatest advantages possible. I am born anew, revitalized, and full of energy.

I am rare and valuable; unique in all the universe. I am nature's greatest miracle in action. I have unlimited potential. I believe in my abilities, attitudes, and goals. I am worthy of greatness because I am the most important person in my world.

Today I push myself to my limits. I use the skills and knowledge from this book every day. I begin the day with a success and end it with a success. My goals are being reached every day and I seek them eagerly.

I act positively and happily, fully accepting myself and others. I live to the fullest by experiencing life without limits. I embrace life. I approach each class, each book, and each assignment with enthusiasm, happiness, and joy. I thirst for knowledge. I look forward to reading and believing this scroll each and every day.

I am a positive and successful student. I know each step I must take to continue to be that way. I am clear on my goals and see myself reaching them. I now realize my infinite potential, thus, my burden lightens. I smile and laugh. I have become the greatest student in the world.

ACKNOWLEDGMENTS

With the assault of the information explosion, it becomes more and more difficult to stay current in one's field. It becomes a necessity to use the research and support of others in writing a book. Although it would be nice to be able to say I created an entirely original book, the truth is that many were involved.

My first thoughts turn to those generous and steadfast associates and friends who gave me the encouragement and support I needed. I am grateful to: Robert Armstrong; Dr. James and Edna Ehleringer; Megan Fraenkel; Mark Huffman; John Koon; Michael and Zaida McDonald; Susie McDowell; Lee, Lisa, Peg and Dr. Norm Pliscou; Dr. Paul Saltman; John Sargent; and Kasey Thornton. I owe a special debt of gratitude to my loving and magnificent father, Dr. Robert Jensen. He has always been an inspiration and model for me.

I am especially beholden to those who helped with specific ideas and guidance, or gave me the feedback from the manuscript I needed so much. I appreciate as special: Bill and Carol Baras, Patricia Franklin, Hans and Gail Heinzerling, and Michael McDonald.

My final words of appreciation are to the three who were undeniably instrumental in this success: my typist, Kathie Schmit, my copy editor, Janet Plate, and of course, Barron's Educational Series, Inc., the progressive publisher who had the courage and wisdom to produce a book needed so badly.

CHAPTER 1

MOTIVATION:

The #1 Place to Start

---

*"There is no such thing as a problem without a gift.
We seek problems because we need their gifts."*

Richard Bach

Over and over again the most common problem mentioned by students is lack of motivation. "I can't seem to get motivated," is a common excuse for almost any school related problem. This chapter explores the reasons for lack of motivation and failure. Then it is followed with twelve ways to motivate yourself to excellence. Once you have understood and completed this chapter, you have taken the first and biggest step toward becoming the success you were meant to be. Read it, and see what reasons have kept you from being a total success.

ELEVEN REASONS FOR LACK OF MOTIVATION

1. Lack of a Definite Goal.

Why are you in school? Is it to become a doctor, lawyer, or engineer? Is it to increase your awareness of current events, real estate, or human nature? Whatever the reason you go to school, you still need to strive for a specific goal. If someone asked you to get into your car and start driving, you'd first say "where to?" There's not much point in getting into your car unless you've got a goal in mind. Your goal may be to go to the store, library, or beach, but you need to know *where* before you start your engine. Students who lack a definite goal will find a weak incentive for excellence and their paths will often stray from the road to success.

2. Laziness.

Often a product of many other factors, laziness is a habit that can cut short even the most promising career. Laziness often stems from negative surroundings, such as critical friends or relatives and a lack of definite goals. Laziness, the opposite of decision and action, is the enemy every successful person must conquer. Successful students use their capacity to reach prompt and definite decisions, and are slow to change their minds. Failures ponder simple decisions endlessly and, even then, change their minds often. Laziness is really the unwillingness to make a decision and the commitment to follow through. Until you have made a strong decision on exactly what your goals are, and committed yourself to achieving them, you can expect failure. Many students have made a strong decision on what they want. But the commitment to these goals is as important as establishing them. It's not enough to say "I want an A in that class." You'll need to say, "I want an A in that class and will get one. I will study ten hours a week if that's what it takes." Therefore, your first decision must be to conquer laziness.

3. Poor Relationships.

Analyze your current relationships with loved ones, family, and friends. Are they positive, encouraging, productive, and helpful? Or are they negative, discouraging, and counterproductive? If you constantly fight with or worry about your mate, you're using up valuable time and energy. How about your mother or father? Are they putting unnecessary pressure upon you to perform in school? You don't need that. Either set them straight that it is *your* life and *your* choices, or learn to cope better with their parenting role. How about your friends? Are they a joy to be with, positive about their lives, and undemanding of your time? If they are not, you need to make some changes. Poor relationships can ruin even the best student.

4. Poor Study Habits.

Each year over one million students drop out of school. In college, only one of three freshmen will graduate. One of the reasons for leaving most often mentioned is, "I can't keep up." Don't fall into the same trap. If your study skills are weak, improve them! There are many ways that you can go about it! Don't write off a career because you can't read or study well. The sad truth is that few schools teach study skills effectively. Some of the most valuable skills such as speed reading, concentration, comprehension, memorizing, notetaking, and analysis

AVOID OVERWORRY!

"When you worry
excessively you can
become paralyzed by an
upcoming event or
obsessed by a current
problem."

are neglected. But they are available from private sources, such as tutors, study groups, and, of course, this book. Learn these skills, and more important, *use* them.

5. Excessive Worry.

Many students waste hours, and even days, fretting and worrying over their school work or personal life. This expends energy that is necessary for other areas. The proper feeling should be concern: a normal, healthy, and necessary caring for what you do. When you worry excessively you can become paralyzed by an upcoming event or obsessed by a current problem. If you can do something about a problem, go do it. If you can't forget it easily, use the method described in the next chapter. It works!

6. Negative Personality Traits.

Of all the years of one's life, those of greatest change are from ages eighteen to twenty-five—the "student" years. As rapid emotional, physical, and social growth takes place, we must make adjustments in our self-image and lifestyle. Those who are unable or unwilling to make the adjustments, unable to "flow with" the changes, may express their frustrations through other outlets. Some of these outlets may be shyness, sarcasm, criticism, withdrawal, guilt, listlessness, or using alibis. All of these negative personality traits can make

A NEGATIVE PERSONALITY WILL SURELY BRING FAILURE . . .

"Negative personality traits can make good study habits difficult or impossible . . . Alibis will always give a poor achiever justification for mediocrity."

---

good study habits difficult or impossible. Ex·
cessive shyness and withdrawn behavior may
lead to criticism by others or unhealthy emotional growth. Sarcasm, though often used in
fun, is a destructive and extremely negative
habit. What's worse is that sarcastic individuals often are unaware of the impact of their
sharp comments. Guilt and criticism often go
together. Highly critical individuals often vent
their guilt feelings through criticism of others,
directing the blame they think they deserve
upon others. There are, of course, countless
alibis that poor students use. Alibis are tools of
those who do not wish to accept responsibility
for their own lives. Alibis will always give a
poor achiever justification for mediocrity. A
student with negative personality traits almost invites failure.

7. Outside Activities.

Everyone has only twenty-four hours in a
day, seven days in a week. Those who try to
cram twenty-five hours into a twenty-four hour
day often become ineffective. Most people try to
do so many things at once that their scattered
efforts cannot possibly be as potent as if all of
their efforts were focused on one activity. The
most common outside activities that inhibit
student progress are belonging to too many
clubs, watching too much television, spending
too much time with friends, and putting in excessive hours at work. Proper budgeting of time
is essential for success.

8.   Lack of Role Models and Support.

It takes a lot to be a great student. There are plenty of heartaches as well as good times. This means that you may need lots of encouragement, support, and acknowledgment to keep you going. Sometimes parents or peers just don't think about how tough it is for you and fail to give you the empathy, self-confidence, and compliments to handle the highs and lows. If this support is not present in your home environment, ask for it. If you don't have a quiet, secluded study area, ask for it. You need it and you deserve it.

9.   Illness.

Doctors and behaviorists estimate an incredible seventy to 95 percent of all illnesses are unintentionally self-induced. The medical term *psychosomatic* includes an endless assortment of illnesses, which include stomachaches, migraine headaches, fevers, and allergies. If you are consistently plagued by any of these illnesses, you need to look at why it happens. If you get a stomachache before studying, are you trying to avoid studying? If your health is not good, look for some reasons why. The reasons may not be purely physical. As children, we learned that being sick allowed us to stay home from school, miss assignments, and get pampered by our parents. There certainly were rewards for being sick, and some of those rewards still exist. You may be doing something similar now, whether consciously or subconsciously. Check your environment to see if there are any payoffs or benefits for your sickness. If so, you may be able to discover the true source of your illness and cure it. Persistent illness can cause missed classes and assignments, encouraging failure.

10. Dull Classes or Uninspiring Teachers

Unfortunately not every teacher you'll have is fun, motivating, dynamic, and committed to your learning. That means some of your classes may be uninteresting or presented in such a way that you either get bored or frustrated. It would be easy to simply blame these teachers so you could get off the hook and have a reason to do poorly. The problem is that you'd still be stuck with the results. Be an active consumer in your education and notice whether you are getting your time's worth in the classroom. If not, it's time to change teachers or classes, or even switch to another school.

11. Conditioned Behavior.

We all are influenced in many ways. The biggest influences on our lives are our peers, television, videos, games, magazines, newspapers, movies, computers, entertainment artists, sports figures, relatives, and parents. *Their* values are communicated to you constantly. And whether you like it or not, many of them become a part of you. But we all get shown just a small part of others' lives. And whereas some rock stars may be living the glamorous life with smiles, money, and groupies, what you don't see is how many failures, rejections, and tough times came first. It's likely that they practiced and disciplined themselves for years to get the fame you see. So, be alert for how you are being influenced and be sure to separate the illusion of easy success from the reality of hard work.

TWELVE STEPS TO ACHIEVING SELF-MOTIVATION

1. Set a Goal.

It is essential that you establish clearly defined goals for yourself. Students who already have a specific goal in mind, such as a career in writing, medicine, acting or law, may need to make their goals more specific. It is not enough to say, "I want to be a scientist." You should decide what field you wish to study and when you plan to enter that field. The time commitment you set up is important. By setting a date for goal completion, you have created a pressure to perform. This self-induced motivation will help you toward your goal by encouraging better decision making. Instead of your being confused and paralyzed by many alternatives, your time commitment will narrow your choices by its limitations. Then you can quickly choose the alternative that takes you toward your goal. Setting personal goals and achieving them can be tremendously satisfying.

Students need to set both long and short range goals for themselves. Short range goals may be those that can be accomplished within two to ten weeks. Such goals must be specific: "I want to get straight A's this term." Longer range goals may be to graduate with highest honors, get a scholarship, or pursue a particular field. Your goals, of course, may include more personal objectives, such as wanting to become more positive, generous, or even to earn a certain amount of money. Remember ninety-eight of one hundred students who are classified as failures had no goal, or specific aim. If you do not know what you want as a goal, find one through experience. Attend lectures, travel, take unusual classes, and meet varied and interesting people. Most students without goals simply have not had enough life experiences to have found what they like. Once you do find what you like, announce your goal to your friends and family. By announcing your goal you'll reinforce its meaning to yourself and you will allow others to encourage and support you. Always broadcast your goals, never your accomplishments or successes. Others will gladly support and applaud your fulfilled dreams. It is finding and setting a goal that is critical.

Whatever the goal, set a long or short range one immediately, so you can begin enjoying the benefits.

Use a self-improvement contract; instead of just talking about goals, set them right now. Decide upon a definite, specific goal for this term in school. What would you like to accomplish? To make the honor roll? To excel in an outside school activity? Become clear on your goal, and write it down on a self-improvement contract like the sample shown in Figure 1. Have a close friend or relative co-sign the contract. Compare your contract to the sample contract to be sure yours is done properly.

First, date it and fill in your name and the "other" person's name. Write the specific goal you wish to accomplish. Then write your agreement. The agreement is how you plan to achieve your goal. What will you do each day or each week that will advance yourself towards your goal? The consequences are rewards if you honor your contract. There are also punishments if you fail to honor it. You should work these out with the person with whom you sign the contract. Make sure you both have something to lose and something to gain. Post your contract in your house as a reminder of the obligation you have to yourself and the co-signer.

The following questions can provide ideas for rewards:
1. What kinds of things do you like to have?
2. What are your major interests?
3. What hobbies do you enjoy most?
4. Whom do you like to spend time with?

5. What do you like to do with those people?
6. What do you do for fun?
7. How do you get away from it all?
8. In what ways do you like to relax?
9. What makes you feel proud or happy?
10. What would be a nice gift to receive?
11. If you just found $5, how would you spend it? How about $10, or even $50?

Now some suggestions:
1. Listening to your favorite music.
2. Eating a favorite fruit or dessert.
3. Reading a great book.
4. Playing tennis or your favorite sport.
5. Camping or escaping for the weekend.
6. Buying music, compact discs, or tapes.
7. Enjoying your favorite meal.
8. Buying yourself or someone you love a gift.
9. Watching TV or renting a video.
10. Going to the beach, mountains, woods, park, or lake.
11. Hanging out with your friends.
12. Getting your hair styled or buying new clothes.
13. Seeing your favorite movie.
14. Eating a midnight snack.
15. Eating at your favorite restaurant.
16. Visiting somewhere different— a play or museum.
17. Doing something creative; writing, building, painting, or taking photos.
18. Taking a short nap.
19. Getting a suntan.
20. Going on an unusual trip.
21. Doing absolutely nothing.
22. Cooking or baking.

Figure 1.
Sample Self-Improvement Contract

_____
Date

Self:_____

Other:_____

AGREEMENT

Self: *I will read or study at least one hour per day. I will use my hand as a pacer and go as quickly as I can. I will also read my Daily Scroll each day.*

Other: *I will encourage Willie to follow his plans and be cheerful, positive, and supportive of his quest for fulfilling his goal.*

CONSEQUENCES

Arranged by Self (if contract is honored): *I will go to my favorite recreational area with my girlfriend.*

(if contract is broken): *I will do extrahouse and yard work for someone else for one week.*

Arranged by Other (if contract is kept): *I agree to take Willie out for dinner of his choice, and buy him two tapes or CDs.*

Signed_____
Self

_____
Other

23. Working in the garden.
24. Skateboarding, skiing, or skating.
25. Visiting friends or relative
26. Going shopping.

2. Build Desire.

Once your goals are formulated, you need to light the fire and begin to fan it. There are several good ways to build a strong desire to fulfill goals. First of all, visualize your goals strongly and clearly every day. Take a minute out of your busy schedule to relax. Close your eyes and picture yourself strongly, vividly, and clearly reaching your goal. Practice this visualization every day, and the desire will build. Desire, like setting a goal, is only the starting point. It is essential to build the desire through affirmation of your specific goal, a definite plan, and then fuel the dreams with the power of your constant and creative imagination. Remember there is no hope for those students who lack the basic desire to excel. They are unlikely to succeed.

3. Think Rationally.

Learn to use your mind constructively and to your advantage all the time. Don't allow yourself to become paralyzed by irrational or unnecessary thoughts. Have an open, receptive, and clear mind, which is free from dogma, superstition, and prejudice. Find out about those things you are not sure of! Do not substitute guesses for thinking. Many students get poor grades because they made incorrect assumptions throughout a course. Don't guess or assume the professor will want something. Ask! Use the power of rational thinking to motivate yourself to new heights. If you're having trouble motivating yourself to do homework, ask yourself if it would be to your benefit to get an *A* in that class. If it would, decide whether you are willing to pay the price. Strike a bargain with yourself. It makes sense to get the best grade you can for the energy you're willing to spend. The skills you are learning from this book will enable you to get top grades at a better "price" (in terms of your own effort).

Once you have established your goals and accepted that you desire them, then the motivation to do homework is necessary. So instead of rationalizing excuses *not* to do something, you can use rational thinking as a reason *to* do something. The power of your rational mind is sufficient to overcome most of your failure-prone habits. Simply stop, and re-evaluate your old beliefs. The following lists will help you see the advantages of good study habits and the disadvantages of not developing them.

Consider the benefits of successful study habits:
1. Studying takes less time.
2. Self-image improves.
3. Gain better comprehension.
4. Less frustration and rereading. Sharpen thinking habits.

5. Better grades.
6. Chances for scholarships.
7. Better qualified for career opportunities.
8. Gain more knowledge.
9. Greater confidence in academic and social area.
10. Explore personal potential.

Consider the cost of <u>not</u> changing study habits:
1. Studying will be time-consuming.
2. Poor self-image.
3. Unnecessary poor comprehension.
4. Discouraging study sessions.
5. Unclear thinking.
6. Poor grades.
7. Less qualified for jobs.
8. Know less material.
9. Lack of self-confidence.
10. Unfulfilled personal potential.
11. Lower chances for getting scholarships.
12. Rational Thinking Builds Success Habits . . .

Consider the "benefits" of poor study habits:
1. Avoid responsibilities and demands from others that require reading skills.
2. Less pressure from others—no risk of failure.
3. Don't threaten others by "outshining" them.
4. Sympathy and attention gained from others who feel sorry for your failures in school.

What is your *rational* decision on study habits?

Suppose that you wish to re-examine your belief that other students get all the breaks and that you'll never graduate with honors. In *Psycho-Cybernetics*, Dr. Maxwell Maltz suggests you ask yourself four important questions:

1. "Is there any rational reason for such a belief?
2. Could it be that I am mistaken in this belief?
3. Would I come to the same conclusion about some other person in a similar situation?
4. Why should I continue to act and feel as if this were true if there is no good reason to believe it?"

Now, scrutinize your belief through these questions and think it out carefully. Most of the time you'll find that your belief holds no factual basis and that it disappears. The power of rational thinking is a powerful tool to use in improving yourself. Don't ignore it. The mind has no limitations except those that you acknowledge.

4. Develop Positive Personality Traits.

Positive personality traits include both attitudes and opinions. A positive person attracts other positive people, thus enabling mutual

A POSITIVE PERSONALITY BRINGS SURE SUCCESS . . .

"If you believe in yourself, you know you can and will succeed in school."

---

support and inspiration. A student with a positive outlook is enthusiastic about life, has a healthy self-image, and makes decisions promptly. This same student is also honest, dependable, and tolerant. A positive personality makes you enjoyable to be with. Start with your attitude. That's simply your relationship with yourself. Do you get along well by yourself, trust yourself, and believe in yourself? If you do believe in yourself, you know you can and will succeed in school. This positive attitude will allow you to handle difficult assignments, demanding teachers, and social pressures. When you are confident and positive, others know they can depend on you. Therefore, they develop confidence in you and can help you reach your goals faster.

If you do not believe in yourself, it is important to change that programming. Read the Daily Scroll and utilize The Secret at the end of the book. A positive personality goes well with a healthy mind and body. Eat lightly. Eat the proper balance of health-giving, wholesome foods. Exercise regularly and learn proper posture. Take care of your hair, teeth, nails, and complexion. Hold your head high and smile. Read as much as you can, informing yourself in fields like philosophy and psychology. Reduce your egotism and replace it with a balance of healthy confidence and modesty. A positive personality is a must for putting into action your desires, plans, and goals.

5. Choose Friends Carefully.

Many students never stop to think about some of the strongest influences on their lives. The people you see the most often affect you the greatest. Most people tend to have a general life-style that is similar to their friends. An important implication is that you'd better choose your friends carefully because in doing so, you choose your future. By associating with those who are your model, you are most apt to make some pleasant changes in yourself.

So if your friends are talented, considerate of others, healthy, happy, and well-rounded, then you are likely to acquire those traits also. Or, if your friends are high achievers who enter science or hobby fairs, become involved in athletics, drama, singing, or good jobs, you'll feel those influences, too.

Yet, the opposite is also true. The saying "Birds of a feather flock together," has been proven accurate. You may acquire some poor habits if your friends are unsupportive, act tough, abuse drugs, drift without goals, or are in legal trouble. These so-called friends can set you back years by leading you away from your own goals.

Friends with positive personalities are strongest in the categories of friendliness, honesty, and communication skills. Friendliness is important because everyone needs good quality friends, and only by being a positive, happy person will you attract good friends.

CHOOSE FRIENDS *CAREFULLY!*

"If your friends are talented, considerate of others, healthy, happy, and well-rounded, then you are likely to acquire those traits also."

Honesty is the cornerstone of a good personality because it is the advertisement of your values. By being honest, you'll avoid embarrassing problems such as having to cover one lie with another—or, worse yet, being confronted with the truth later on. Communication is an essential part of a positive personality because most people do not read minds, and verbal messages are the best we can do. Be direct, honest, and square with your thoughts and feelings. It will save many headaches later on and help you earn the healthy respect of others.

If a friend is not a positive experience for you and much of the time you have disagreements, you need to make some changes. Either spend less time with that friend, or figure out how to get along better. It's important to have a confidant or study partner, or maybe one person who is both. But if you have a specific goal to reach, and if this "friend" is constantly pouring out his or her problems to you and infringing upon your peace of mind or time, wake up! You don't have to stay in any relationship, regardless of whether or not that person "needs" you. Regardless of his or her needs, this "friend" does not have the right to ruin your happiness or your chance of reaching your goal. A good schoolmate can be a dynamic source of inspiration, knowledge, and enjoyment. By choosing positive, growing friends you will find the path much easier. But most agree, it is necessary to choose your friends carefully.

6.　Have Faith in Yourself.

The starting point for success in school, even before goals and desire, is trust. If you don't believe in yourself, there's no point in trying, is there? Self-trust and faith are essential. "If you think you're beaten, you are," means those without faith in themselves will surely fail. Faith is the basis of all miracles and the basis for all success. You must believe in this essential fact: What the mind can conceive and believe, it can achieve. People have used their faith and mind to stop their own heartbeat, walk on hot coals, and stop from bleeding. So it can certainly be used more effectively to get *A's*.

Maybe you've been thinking that you need that "something extra" to succeed. Do you think you lack tools, resources, opportunity, creativity or intelligence? Forget that negative thinking. You have not been shortchanged! Let's take inventory to find out what you really have going for you.

Your marvelous eyes have a hundred million sensory receptors with which to enjoy the world. You can watch a sunset, read a book, or see a loved one. Count one asset!

And through the courtesy of a complex, well-engineered hearing system you can listen beautifully. You can hear a concert, a waterfall, or a friendly voice. Count another asset!

Your trained voice can speak any language in the world. You can laugh, whisper, or shout for joy. Count another asset!

Your incredible body has over 500 muscles,

200 bones, and 60 miles of veins and arteries to serve you. Yet it tirelessly builds thousands of new cells daily and features a heart which beats over 100,000 times and pumps over 4,000 gallons a day without complaint. Count yet another asset!

Do you complain of a lack of wealth? Your personal wealth is endless! What rich man, old and feeble would not gladly exchange all his money, property, gold, stocks, and bonds for the blessings you have taken for granted? To create a computer nearly equal to your brain, it would cost over $10 billion. Don't treat yourself lightly! It would take up as much space as the Empire State Building and require the water of the Mississippi River just to cool it. You master-mind a $10 billion super computer, which features memory banks, creativity, and logic components. It controls millions of pain, touch, and temperature detectors all over your body, which can help you adjust to burning deserts, the sea, polar ice caps, outer space, and even classes at school.

You are the greatest creation the world has ever seen. You are the technological pinnacle of mankind. Your list of personal assets is endless and you must acknowledge those treasures to become successful. Never again complain that you need "something extra." You are one-of-a-kind and unique among the 70 billion humans who have ever lived. Enjoy the rarity you have. Use your assets to become the student you know you can be.

You can develop faith in yourself by accepting yourself as you are and as the person you can become. The preceding paragraphs and your Daily Scroll will help you if you read them often. If you ever lacked faith about your potential as a student, the fears will diminish. The mind will accept as truth anything, if it is repeated and reinforced enough.

Develop confidence and faith in yourself through actions. Set up short, easily attainable goals for yourself and watch your successes pile up. Then focus your memory and present thoughts on your virtues. This gives a stronger picture of yourself, thus building faith also.

7. Give Reinforcement.

The best way to get more of what you want is to reward the source when the desired behavior is produced. This is known as positive reinforcement. Set up a reward system for yourself for long and short term goals. When you accomplish a short term goal, such as getting an *A* on a midterm, reward yourself with something you value. You may want to give yourself a dinner, a concert, a day at the beach, an item of clothing, or a record. Be fair to yourself and reward yourself when you achieve your goal. Rewards are the whole principle behind the self-improvement contract introduced earlier in this chapter. Reward the positive and, if appropriate, punish the negative.

One mistake many people make when trying to use a reward system is delaying the rewards or offering them at intervals too great to be effective. Set up a reward system that can be administered at short intervals. Never more than a week should pass without at least some temporary rewards. When used properly, a program of positive reinforcement can bring about the desired habits with ease.

8. Get Specialized Skills.

You can be a great student if you have the skills, information, confidence, and motivation to do it. If you need more than this book provides, take some specialized courses. Sign up for courses in memory and study skills, speed reading, and test preparation. Learn from others who do it well. Discipline yourself to learn the habits you need to have to be a total success. Although you always can find someone who will tell you how hard school is or how tough certain classes are, ignore him or her. There are just as many others who juggle a full load of classes *and* have time for fun. It can be done; you just need to know how to do it. So, make your plans now to fill in your study gaps and start enjoying school.

9. Use Special "Mind-motivators"

Motivation can be easy if you know how it works. You know you are motivated already to do things. After all, you got out of bed this morning, showered, got dressed, ate, and now you are reading this book. "Big deal," you say, "anyone can do that." You're right. Except for one thing. This means your brain (that's you!) *already* knows how to get you to do things. And the same things that get you motivated to do those ordinary things can also motivate you to do things like homework!

It's simply a matter of finding out what your brain does to put you in motion. And that's pretty simple. But it'll take a bit of research on your part. Simply read this section all the way through, then go back and actually do the instructions.

Close your eyes and think about an activity that you're very motivated to do. Pick something that you constantly overcome obstacles to get yourself to do, such as working out, sports practice, a concert, a big date, preparing for something, or going on a vacation. While you are thinking about yourself doing that activity, hold it in your mind.

What kinds of feelings (if any) do you have about doing that item? Where are those feelings located and what's the intensity of them? Do you hear any sounds that get you motivated to do something? Is there a voice (do you tell yourself "Now is the time!")? What are the qualities of that sound? Close up; faraway? Which direction is that sound coming from? Low, high, fast, or slow? If you have a picture in your mind of doing that activity, are you seeing youself "over there" in the picture or are you seeing the incident out of your own eyes, in the moment of doing it? Is it a movie or a still frame? Is the activity close up or faraway? In color or in black and white? Is it in 3-D or flat two-dimensional? Consider each of those qualities, then make up a list.

Your list is a record of how your brain motivates you to do something. As an example, you might find that when you are highly motivated to do something, you "hear" a loud booming voice coming from above your right ear, then you see the positive outcome in 3-D, running like a color movie, and you are associated *in* the experience of doing it. Now, that's just an example. Your list of "motivational" brain qualities might be different, but it's worth its weight in gold to you.

Take the item that you've had trouble getting yourself motivated to do. Let's say it's studying or doing your homework. Now add the things that motivate you to do the *new* activity. That means that if color motivates you, add color. If moving action motivates you, add that. If a voice motivates you, add that. Make all the changes from your earlier list. You'll discover that some of the qualities affect you more than others. Keep adding those qualities; you'll feel the difference if you are doing this correctly.

What you're actually doing is adding your brain's representation of "motivation" to an item that you previously were unmotivated to do. Complete the visualization and you'll know how you get motivated and how your brain can be used to do it at will. In a sense, you have gone from being a passenger on the "bus of life" to being the driver. That's pretty exciting!

10. Solve Personal Problems.

If personal situations are on your mind, it is difficult to concentrate, even with good study skills. Car problems, poor health, or romantic involvements are a part of life, but there is no reason why these should dominate. The student years are often the most traumatic portion of one's life. It seems that everything that could happen, does. But outside events don't have to be catastrophes if you keep them in perspective. Most are really not the disasters they are made out to be.

One mistake consistently made in dealing with personal problems is avoiding them because of "overthinking." This means making assumptions about what we perceive will or will not happen. These assumptions often immobilize an otherwise clear thinking individual. Don't assume there is a problem, but confront the person involved. Try to clear it up early. Be direct, honest, and warm. Communicate your feelings first, then your thoughts. Listen to the other side before deciding upon a course of action. But take the situation into your hands and deal with it. Avoiding it only postpones it and amplifies the problem. Make an effort to not "overthink" or avoid personal problems, and they will become less worry for you.

Most personal conflicts go away in time, but it's rarely worth it to wait that long. Almost every school has a qualified counseling staff that can help you to solve difficult problems.

Chances are good that they have already dealt with and solved problems very similar to yours.

11. Develop Persistence.

Consider the following proverb:

Nothing in the world can take the place of persistence.
Talent will not, nothing is more common than unsuccessful men with talent.
Genius will not, unrewarded genius is almost a proverb.
Education will not, the world is full of educated derelicts.
Persistence and determination alone are omnipotent.

Whereas motivation is essential to begin the path to success, only persistence will keep you on the path. Motivation is like fuel for your car; it gets you going toward your goal. But cars will run out of gas unless the persistence is there to refuel. The starting point for developing persistence is to have something to persist toward. Have an exact and desirable goal in mind and keep it there. Your motivation will move you to action, but your persistence will keep you moving. Persistence is insured, provided these six qualities are developed.

Desire. Essential to success is the intense desire for achievement. A strong desire indicates your willingness to persist in making

PERSISTENCE!

"While motivation is essential to begin the path to success, only persistence will keep you on the path."

sacrifices to reach your goal. Your strong desire will help put you in the right place at the right time. Finally, your strong desire will keep the bonfires of persistence burning.

Self-reliance. Confidence in yourself will allow you to be persistent. You must have exceptional faith in your own abilities because you will be tried and tested many times on your path to success. You must learn to rely on yourself because there is no one else to rely on. You may fail dozens of times, but your next effort may bring a success. You'll never know how close success is until you take that one extra step. You were not born a failure nor will you become one. One step at a time, and only one step at a time, is necessary. You may liken yourself to an acorn that becomes a mighty tree and eventually builds a forest. Countless success stories arose from failures who refused to give up. Your confidence will help strengthen the persistence you need.

Reinforcement. There are three excellent ways to reinforce your persistence. One way is to keep exact goals posted conspicuously where you live, work, and drive. You should see reminders of your goals everywhere you go. If your goal is to get into Harvard Law School, get a picture of it and put that picture in your bathroom, on your refrigerator door, or on the dashboard of your car. This reinforcement will help your subconscious mind work towards that goal. It will help remind you of the goal you are striving for.

A second way to reinforce your persistence is through successes. Set temporary, short, easily attainable goals and meet them. the more successes you gain, the greater the personal ego reinforcement. It's difficult to lack confidence when you are being successful each and every day.

You can receive reinforcement a third way—from positive friends. Encouraging, supportive and enthusiastic friends can help inspire and push you along the path to success. So be sure to chose your friends carefully, as they can and will influence your success patterns.

Mastery of Habits. Self-control is another essential step toward persistence. You must become the true master of your own personal habits. Negative habits such as overindulgence, poor health, criticizing others, financial mismanagement, or poor use of time can be lessened and maintained at less destructive levels. To help self-control, post positive reminders such as notecards in your house with your new habits written down. By constant reminder and desire, you'll be able to control those poor habits.

Courage. Every successful person must have the personal courage and conviction of faith to maintain persistence. You must ignore criticism from others and keep your own plans and goals in mind. It will take courage to maintain a positive nature while others fire the arrows of negativism and criticism. Read the Daily Scroll each day, and it will affirm your goals and beliefs, giving you the courage you need to act positively.

Accountability. One of the quickest paths to failure is justifying or placing blame. You might justify low performance by saying others (not just you) are doing poorly, you were sick, or the class was boring. Or, you may lay blame and say the teacher is a hard grader. And all of those reasons may be true. The question is whether those reasons can motivate or mobilize you to improve. Usually they don't. You still get the same results. In life, you either have results or you have reasons (the stories and justifications that explain the results). Why not just get the results you want?

Positive Mental Attitude. A crucial step toward maintaining persistence is to have strong personal optimism. Keep your mind tightly closed against negative people and thoughts. Eliminate negative words from your vocabulary such as impossible, can't, won't, defeat, failure, or unworkable. Do not allow yourself to think about the negative side of things. A positive mental attitude means you are confident of your own ability to succeed, and you refuse to associate with those who think otherwise.

Think, believe, and act in a positive manner. There is no substitute for a continuous effort. The schools are full of students who make half-hearted efforts, and who end up with poor grades and an incomplete, inadequate education. The most common reasons for lack of persistence are lack of intense desire for a specific goal and lack of faith in yourself. Many people are too easily discouraged by failures. Many begin to see themselves as failures simply because they were not successful at some specific task. But *you* are not a failure, no matter how many times you do not live up to your expectations. Thomas Edison said he had nearly 10,000 failures on the path to producing the electric light bulb. Did he give up? Of course not, and he said he didn't mind failure at all because he learned from every one. Each failure taught him how *not* to do it the next time. In school, learn from your tests. When you get a low grade, find out why, so you can prepare better for the next test. Continuous, applied effort, without giving up, is a sure way to become successful. Successful students lead the parade of fulfillment, achievement, and happiness while the unsuccessful sit on the sidelines. Most students show sporadic promise in school, but the achievers have made the consistent effort through their willpower. The achievers begin with strong desire for an exact purpose, continue with faith in themselves, and then follow through with the habit of using willpower.

A success will not give up. He or she will explore and exhaust all possibilities and alternatives. Many problems go unsolved because someone gave up and lost the desire to continue. A genius does not wait for a magical bolt of inspiration. It takes hard work and long hours to produce. Edison rightly said, "Genius is one percent inspiration and ninety-nine percent perspiration." And he should know. He holds more U.S. patents than any other man. Yet, he experienced thousands of failures in his career. So be willing to invest your time and energy—ideas don't work unless you do.

12. Take Action.

Every desire, every plan, every bit of knowledge is useless unless followed by action. No battle plan has ever won a war, no law ever prevented a crime, no book ever read itself. Action is the key. Repeat it to yourself over and over again. Action is the key. Do not wait for tomorrow. Tomorrow may never come. Do not wait for the time to be right. The time is right now. Do not worry about what to do, or how to do it. Just say when. Say now. Begin this moment. This precious moment, which will never come again. This priceless day, which will end in just a few hours, must be utilized. Live each day to the fullest through action. Would you be proud to say how you spent today, maybe the last of your life? Put your alibis and excuses away. Open up your eyes, your heart, your mind. Embrace life, laugh, and have fun. But most of all, act, and act now. Action is the only thing that will reap the rewards you want. It's the single most potent ingredient to success. Do not delay. You have but one life, and you must not waste today, possibly the last and most precious day of your life. Make today the culmination of your desires, plans, and knowledge. Act now and become a successful student.

REVIEW THESE POINTS

Eleven Reasons for Failure

1. Lack of a definite goal.
2. Laziness.
3. Poor relationships.
4. Poor study habits.
5. Excessive worry.
6. Negative personality traits.
7. Outside activities.
8. Lack of role models and support.
9. Illness.
10. Dull classes or inspiring teachers.
11. Conditioned behavior.

Twelve Steps to Achieving Self-Motivation

1. Set a goal.
2. Build desire.
3. Think rationally.
4. Develop positive personality traits.
5. Choose friends carefully.
6. Have faith in yourself.
7. Give reinforcement.
8. Get specialized skills.
9. Use special "mind-motivators."
10. Solve personal problems.
11. Develop persistence.
12. Take action.

Figure 2.
Sample Notes* for Chapter 1

*See pages 103–107 for a description of how to prepare creative notes like these.

CHAPTER 2

SUCCESS HABITS:

Begin Now

"In brief, sir, study what you most affect."
                              Shakespeare

SUCCESSFUL SCHOOL HABITS

In 1912 Harry Wilson wrote an interesting story named "Bunker Bean." It's the saga of a man who was tricked into believing in himself. Bunker was a man who was penniless and orphaned as a child. As an adult, he lived in a cheap boarding house suffering a life of frustration and poverty. But a false spiritualistic medium moved into his boarding house and convinced him to give up part of his wages in exchange for psychic readings. The psychic told Bunker that life progressed in vast karmic cycles and that although Bunker's life was very negative, he was completing the lower half of a cycle. The upcoming portion of his life was to be the exact opposite and he was to take on the successful qualities of Napoleon. Bunker believed the psychic and began assuming the virtues of his new role model. After reading and following books on Napoleon, Bunker became such a success that his friends and employer could hardly believe the changes. Over a period of time the new success habits became such a part of him that even when he found out the psychic was a fake, it didn't matter. His successful habits had become a permanent part of his life.

The point of the story is that once successful habits are formed, they will be with you until you form new ones. In school, the successful habits you learn and use now will benefit you later in life. So, let's look at some of the important habits for school success.

1. Know Thyself.

If you wanted to get inside a valuable locked container wouldn't you want to know the combination to the lock? Of course you would. Yet many students study and try to get at the "riches of knowledge" using the wrong approach or "combination" to their lock.

A learning style is a preferred way to learn. You may have noticed that, given a choice, you'd choose one way of learning over another: to listen, watch, or actually try something out. In other words, would you rather have someone tell you about a subject, read or watch a movie about it, or go experience it happening, like in a science lab? These three styles respectively are examples of auditory, visual, or kinesthetic learning. But there are other ways to categorize how you learn.

You may be more *inductive* (specific concrete examples needed first, such as: "Have you ever been in a car that ran out of gas?") or *deductive* (abstract global overview preferred first, such as: "I'm going to talk to you about transportation; how we get from A to B and what causes breakdowns."). A teacher who talks about specific examples may be much more interesting to you than one who tries to relate the subject to significant trends and major global issues.

Another learning style is your orientation towards time. You may respond more to the present, or maybe the past, or even the future. A teacher who talks to you about your long-term goals may totally lose your attention whereas another who talks about getting out of class early may get your attention. And there are other learning styles, too. But those are enough for the moment.

The point is simple. Start paying attention to how you learn best and begin to use that way to learn. You don't need to struggle or learn slowly. You are too bright for that. Learning takes very little time. It's all the time wasted *not* learning that adds up to most students' study time. Learn your own "learning lock combination" by trial and error, test and retest. Go with your strengths. Honor your resources and enjoy the results.

2. Prepare Yourself.

Start your school day by putting forth your best effort. Check over your personal appearance. Research confirms that first impressions are usually correct. So, make the first impression a good one. Wear clothes that reinforce your image as a student and learner. Conservative, academic styles often impress instructors on a subconscious, if not conscious level. In many schools, a teacher would be much more favorably impressed by a student in a dressy outfit carrying a briefcase than one in a sweatshirt, jeans and sandals. Appropriate clothing certainly can help you feel better and enhance your self-image. Make sure you have the books, papers, and other supplies you'll need for class.

3. Improve Your Self-image.

How do you see yourself? Do you think of yourself as a good or poor student? One of the most dramatic psychological discoveries of the twentieth century has been the uncovering of the "self-image." Whether you realize it or not, all of your actions, feelings, and behavior are consistent with your conception of yourself. The beautiful thing about that fact is it can be changed. There are thousands of students who see themselves as poor students, feel that way, hang around other poor students, and consequently become failures. Why? They "prove" themselves right by becoming the failures they thought they were.

Don't confuse self-image with positive thinking. They are not the same. Positive thinking is believing that things will turn out well whether it's plausible or not. But by improving your self-image, you are getting at the source, the only thing you have true control over: yourself. So, starting today, begin picturing yourself as a good student. The purpose of a creative mental picture is simple. First, it enables you to see the end product, and thereby become comfortable with the "new you." Whatever kind of person you would like to be or whatever changes you would like to make, the change has to come from within. By becoming comfortable with the "future" you, your subconscious can begin to direct your thoughts and actions accordingly. Your new mental picture can actually provide

IMPROVE YOUR SELF-IMAGE!

"Whether you realize it
or not, all of your
actions, feelings, and
behavior are consistent with
your conception of yourself . . .
So, starting today, begin
picturing yourself as a
good student."

you with a "mental mold" or model for your actions by keeping the desired behavior in mind.

You will become what you think about, dream about, and desire to be the most. Benjamin Franklin said we should practice what we wish to become, not what we are. That's the second benefit of mental pictures. You can become the person for whom you act out the role. Most of us have already done this role-playing in one form or another. Often movie actors find that by playing one role for too long, they actually do take on characteristics of that role. Playing a role can actually help you become it!

Proper mental picturing takes about two minutes a day. Sit or lie comfortably, and close your eyes. Use your imagination to create a strong, clear picture of yourself doing the desired behavior. Make the picture alive, imagining the sights and sounds of yourself successfully studying. Picture yourself zipping through a textbook, giving a great report in class, or getting an *A* on a test. Sound strange? Remember this: if you can't even imagine yourself getting *A*'s, what hope is there for the real thing?

To become an *A* student you have got to believe it's possible for you first. Associate with other good students and acquire the study skills taught in this book. Miracles will begin as soon as you see yourself as an *A* student because you *are* one when you believe in yourself.

4. Use Visualization Techniques.

Sit in a relaxed position and close your eyes. Imagine a huge chalkboard in your mind. Fill the chalkboard with pictures of your concerns, problems, and worries. Get a vivid picture and hold it for a few seconds. Now, in your imagination, pick up an eraser. Beginning in the upper left hand corner of the chalkboard, slowly erase all your problems. Sometimes it requires you to "press hard" or "erase" over again in your imagination, but it always clears the problems from your head.

Another effective technique involves using a piece of notepaper. These four steps are important to follow exactly:

1. Write down a description of your most pressing problem.
2. Write down at least two possible solutions to the problem. There is always more than one solution, so think hard until you come up with some alternative actions to take.
3. Write down exactly when you plan to do something about the problem. On what date and at what time do you plan to imple ment your solutions?
4. Fold the piece of paper in half. While you are still looking at it, put it away in a desk or drawer.

This system has the advantage of taking the problem out of your head, removing the worry of what to do, and eliminating the decision of when to do it. Let the paper carry the burden of the problem. Once you can eliminate unnecessary or negative thoughts, your mind can focus on more urgent or scholastic matters.

5. Read Extensively.

Superior students are not always rapid readers, but they read extensively, with excellent comprehension. You don't need a high IQ to read well. In fact, 70 percent of all poor readers have an average or above-average IQ. It's necessary to be a good reader because you will get 75 percent of all your information from printed material. A useful guideline is this: If your grades are low, the first thing to suspect is poor reading skills. It's not difficult to improve them, provided you seek qualified help. Once you're satisfied with your reading skills, use them. Read as much as you can, and read material with varying levels of difficulty. It's not enough to read the morning newspaper if you want to be really well read. Read textbooks, nonfiction best sellers, and magazines. The important thing is to read as much as you can.

6. Eat Intelligently.

Your diet strongly affects your moods, energy levels, and thinking ability. By taking better care of the inside of yourself, you can increase your chances for success on your report card.

Stay with a low sugar, low salt, and low fat diet. Eat several small meals a day instead of fewer large meals. Drink six to eight glasses of pure water each day (soft drinks don't count). Avoid foods that upset your system. Drink very little liquids with your meals. Instead, eat food higher in water content such as salads, vegetables, and pasta. Eat at least one-half of your vegetables fresh and uncooked. Keep whole grains and natural foods in your diet. Cook foods with more herbs, lemon juice, and spices, and less salt. Eat slowly.

Need an energy boost? Get your sugars from fructose, the sugar in fruits. Eat a banana, apple, peach, pear, tangerine, orange, or kiwi fruit. Need to relax? A high carbohydrate meal with calcium (milk or other dairy product) will calm you by raising your levels of tryptophan and serotonin, both calm-inducers. Peanuts do the same.

If you need to do a lot of studying and thinking, there's a science to it. Neurotransmitters—the brain's chemical messengers—are created from the protein in your food. Make sure that you have enough protein (and the right kinds) for healthy thinking. Before studying, eat a light protein-rich meal possibly with eggs, turkey and fish. To remember what you study, eat foods that help the release of CCK (cholecystokinin)—tryptophan, choline, and phenylalanine—neurotransmitters associated with memory. These include milk, nuts, bananas, seeds, rice, and oats.

7. Attend Class Regularly.

There are two cases when missing class can be beneficial. The first is when you urgently need that time to prepare for an exam or write a paper, and the second is when ill health makes it inadvisable to attend. Regular attendance assures you'll have all the necessary lecture notes for exams and allows you the opportunity to clarify your understanding of any textbook reading while it's still fresh in your mind.

Get to class on time. It irritates teachers when late students interrupt their lectures. It is advisable to bring some assignment or reading to class in case the teacher is late. Then you can still make good use of your time. Arriving early will also allow you to get the seat you want near the front of the class. Sitting in the front will help you hear more easily, see visual aids clearly, and show your teacher you're more interested in the class.

8. Know Your Teacher.

See your teacher after class and develop a friendship if possible. Clear up difficult points from class lectures and give your teacher feedback on lecture material and presentation. Most instructors really appreciate knowing how well their material is coming across.

It's often beneficial to find out your teacher's

preferences. What is his or her favorite subject or author? At one university, an American literature professor reportedly never gave A's to undergraduates. An ambitious sophomore talked to him after class and found out that his favorite author was Theodore Dreiser. He had prepared his doctoral dissertation on Dreiser. So the student matched strengths, reading and researching as much as he could on Dreiser. The final exam he wrote (on Dreiser, of course) was so interesting to him and well presented that he earned the only A in the class. In short, specialize your approach by appealing to what your professor likes. Not only will it help your grades, but you will learn much more.

9. Make a Schedule if It Helps.

There is no relationship between a strict schedule and good grades. Just as many A students have strict schedules as have no schedules. Should you use a schedule? If you have a tendency to procrastinate, use one. Those who need schedules will find that they can pinpoint effective times for study. A schedule can help remind you of your school commitments and prevent careless oversights.

A weekly study schedule should be a general list of your major time commitments. Include classes, athletics, work schedules, or social engagements. Keep this weekly schedule to insure the obvious is not forgotten. Then keep a daily appointment, errand, and "to do" list of smaller commitments. At the end of the day, cross off those things you've completed, and carry the remaining tasks over to the next day. This really increases goal orientation and builds your success image through daily achievement.

10. Develop Concentration.

Find the right time for study. Do it when you are most efficient and receptive to information, not when a schedule says so. Some students are "night" people, those who are just getting ready to study around midnight, whereas others prefer daylight. Find the proper place for studying by using the same desk each time if possible. The same desk creates familiarity and comfort, which aids in getting started each time.

If you want to be outstanding in any field, there is one important rule to observe: Concentrate. Get one thing in your mind and heart and bloodstream. Put side blinders on your eyes so you cannot see all the distractions and temptations along the way. Forget the sidelines, and then put all the steam you've got right on the piston head and drive with full power down the main track. Keep out of the mud puddles; stay on the rails. Keep off the detours and sidings and drive straight ahead without continual startings and stoppings. Keep your mind on what you are doing. That helps create a good

CONCENTRATE YOUR EFFORTS!

"If you want to be
outstanding in any field,
there is one inmportant
rule to observe:
'concentrate.'"

"mental set" for studying. Remove the usual distractions such as a phone, calendar of upcoming events, television, and pinups. Anything you have that stimulates daydreaming will destroy your concentration. The ideal noise for study is "white noise," a term used to describe a low-level background sound that masks outside distractions. Ideally, you can use instrumental music, a bubbling aquarium, or even a steady traffic flow. These noises help equalize the extremes of dead quiet and unbearable annoyances.

Set realistic study goals. Don't tell yourself, "I'm not getting out of this chair until I know this chemistry book." Rather, set a realistic goal such as, "I'm going to learn chapters six and seven within an hour." Focus energy on just one topic at a time.

It takes special concentration to eliminate the mental clutter that often impairs good study habits. Any obvious impediment to concentration should be removed. Before concentration is automatic, take care of any immediate needs such as hunger.

11. Reduce Study Stress.

Anticipate deadlines and complete papers and projects well in advance. This serves the dual purpose of insuring assignment completion and allowing for the possibility of its review or revision. If your paper is due on the sixteenth, finish it by the tenth or twelfth. Then, if your schedule suddenly gets crowded

DREAM YOUR WAY TO SUCCESS!

"In the subconscious or dream state, your mind can re-sort, recreate, and review material so that it becomes even more powerful and clear the next morning. Study or review immediately before sleeping."

or hectic, there's no anxiety getting it in on time. And if you get any new ideas, you'll have time to include them in your assignment.

Take advantage of your subconscious mind. A good student studies before sleeping because the mind can use the dream state to rework your material. Many famous inventions have been discovered through dreams. In the subconscious or dream state, your mind can re-sort, recreate, and review material so that it becomes even more powerful and clear the next morning. Study or review immediately before sleeping. Then tell yourself that you wish to dream about it. In time, you'll be literally dreaming your way to success.

12. Choose an Appropriate Study Area.

It helps to study in familiar places each time because it enables you to develop a quick consistent pattern for concentration. Otherwise you may spend the first twenty minutes of your study time getting familiar with a new desk, chair, room scenery, and passersby. Generally, it's not advisable to study on your bed because it's so comfortable; you may end up sleeping instead of studying. Study in an area where the lighting is indirect, yet strong; it should also be reasonably quiet. Make sure the book you are reading is 14 to 18 inches from your eyes. By your keeping your book at this distance, eye fatigue will be lessened.

SELECT A PROPER STUDY AREA!

"It helps to study in
familiar places because
it enables you to
develop a quick,
consistent pattern for
concentration."

Two things you can do to help spend your study time more efficiently are setting study goals and allowing a study recess. Be sure to set short, easily attainable goals. Every hour, take a five minute break for refreshments or to walk around in order to increase circulation. You'll find your concentration much improved.

13. Psych Yourself Into Study Readiness

Prestudy blues kill more good intentions because a poor attitude can be devastating. Instead of complaining, tell yourself, "I'm going to get this material and get it fast." Decide on what you need to learn and in how much time it will take you to cover the required material. If you approach your task with a positive, receptive, open mind, you will go much faster. If you *believe* you can move through the text rapidly, half the battle is won.

There are an almost unlimited number of distractions that mysteriously pop up just before studying. At times, studying seems so boring that almost anything is more interesting. Learn to avoid such prestudy tactics as preparing a snack, staring at the ceiling, or feeling the desire to visit friends. Your studying will become easier and easier. Most things are done out of habit, not out of need, so think about whether you really need those usual rituals. Form consistent positive study habits of getting assigned work done on time. Only then will you become the master of your school habits.

14. Study "Bite-sized" Chunks

One of the great "stoppers" to getting started is the amount of studying to do. After all, who wants to sit down to study for two or three hours on a beautiful day? The answer is simple, if you keep this statement about the brain in mind: It is easier to "act your way" into feeling than to "feel your way into acting" a certain way.

An Olympic athlete realized this and had a solution. On cold winter mornings, he rarely felt like getting up to work out. So he said, "I'll get dressed, then see how I feel." He put on his sweatshirt and sweatpants. Then he felt okay, so he put on his running shoes. After that, he still felt okay, so he put on his gloves and wool hat. Then he said, "I'll just take a short walk." So he started out. After a while, the cold invigorating morning air awakened him even more. So he began to run. The more he ran, the more loose and energetic he felt. In a short time, he was up to full speed and promptly completed his workout. The funny part is this: he *never* felt like doing it—he only felt okay at each step along the way!

That means that it is better to start doing a small chunk of homework than to wait for a bolt of inspiration out of the blue. That "bolt" rarely happens. If you've got two chapters to do, just promise yourself that you'll do an overview.

Then, at the end of the overview, if you're getting into it, do more.

Above all, don't let yourself get discouraged by thick books or imposing titles. Set up short, easily attainable goals and count your successes as you move unhesitatingly through even the toughest material. Almost any material can be broken up into a format style. Separate difficult reading into categories, for example, introduction, examples, background, opinions, and facts. Then the material will become much more readable.

One step at a time. Inch by inch, it's a cinch. Nothing big and grand needed. Just bite off a small, chewable chunk and do it. No excuses, no procrastination. Begin your work now and it'll get done.

15. Put Balance in Your Life

At this time of your life, you've got a lot to juggle: academics, fitness, relationships, family, chores, school activities, finances, hobbies, and health. One thing you can be sure of is this: life requires that you pay attention to every part of it. If you ignore your health, you can almost expect illness. If you ignore your relationships, you can expect upsets. And it's the same for each of the other areas.

The moral is simple. Organize your activities. Make sure you set aside time to play, time to work out, time for planning, time for homework, and time for friends and family. Take care of tickets, promises, and commitments.

Life offers much, but it demands much, too. Plan your work and work your plan. Anything less will come back to you in the form of trouble. But if you stand up to the challenge, you'll enjoy lower stress and more fun every day.

16. Make the Best of School.

An important attribute of good students is a strong interest in school. If you aren't interested in your classes, either you shouldn't be taking them, or you should try to generate some interest in them. Normally, interest is an automatic factor, but if it is not so with you, check over the previous chapter on motivation. Set a goal and stick to it. Students with interest in their courses invariably do better in them. Meet other students and share interests with them. In almost every subject you study, you can find some aspect that interests you. The knowledge you build from that interest leads to good grades and fosters more interest. One of the worst enemies of poor students is low morale and feelings of hopelessness. By becoming interested in your classes, classmates, and professors you will generate more morale and enthusiasm. This will help you want to do well and help you have more fun in school.

A really amazing study was done on prisoners of war who were in brutal, isolated conditions for years at a time. It turns out that some of them were, as you might expect, emotional "basket cases" by the time of their release. But the exceptions were quite a study in how to cope. These prisoners in horrendous conditions adopted a "one day at a time" and "I refuse to let them get me down" attitude. They had chosen to be in charge, to be the captains of their own fate, and to choose whether or not they were going to have a good day or not.

This philosophy is especially important in school. You may have a heavy study load, dull teachers, and inedible cafeteria food. The weather may be poor, your home life may be rough, and your love life may be nonexistent. But simply refuse to let others decide what kind of day you'll have. It's not what happens in life, it's what you do about what happens that counts. Rise above the tough times; you'll need to develop that winner's attitude—you've got a lot of good years ahead of you. The job you want, the relationships you want, and the life you want will require that you be a bigger person. If the circumstances don't suit you, go out and make ones that do suit you. Be happy, not because you have some outside reason, but because you choose it—from the inside.

REVIEW THESE POINTS

Success Habits

1. Know thyself.
2. Prepare yourself.
3. Improve your self-image.
4. Use visualization techniques.
5. Read extensively.
6. Eat intelligently.
7. Attend classes regularly.
8. Know your teacher.
9. Make a schedule if it helps.
10. Develop concentration.
11. Reduce study stress.
12. Choose an appropriate study area.
13. Psych yourself into "study readiness."
14. Study "bite-sized" chunks.
15. Put balance in your life.
16. Make the best of school.

Figure 3
Sample Notes* for Chapter 2

*See pages 103–107 for a description of how to prepare creative notes like these.

CHAPTER **3**

ATTACK PLAN FOR STUDYING:

A New Approach

Whatever the mind of man can conceive and believe it can achieve."

Napoleon Hill

An average student has spent over 22,000 hours studying from the time he or she began school through the twelfth grade. This enormous amount of time can be reduced considerably through dynamic study skills. But most students are never really taught how to study. It's a process the schools expect students to learn on their own. And because it is not usually taught, *this is the most important chapter in the book for you*. This dynamic study process will help you every time you open a textbook from now on. Learn it and use it.

Efficient studying does not simply consist of reading, underlining, and rereading. Your new study process consists of reading, writing, thinking, and recalling. It is based on the multilayered learning process and actually takes less time than your old method of study. It may seem longer at first, but each step takes less time, and because it is so well structured, you will have better recall at test time. The following is the explosive, surefire study process you need!

Study for Straight A's by P-A-G-E: 1) Prepare, 2) Ask, 3) Gather, and 4) Evaluate

Time and again students have proved that a multilayered study process is much more effective than spending all your time reading and highlighting. The only way to learn the material is to become actively involved in absorbing and integrating it. Study reading is an active process, not a passive one. So get out your texts and some notepaper: you're ready to learn!

1. <u>Prepare</u> for Reading by Browsing Through Your Texts.

Survey to get an overview of the book, turning pages quickly so that you spend about two minutes to gather the information that answers the following questions:

1. What are the main topics?
2. What do I already know about these topics?
3. What special terminology is used to present the topics?
4. Who is the author?
5. How is the book organized?
6. How difficult is the material and how difficult is the presentation?

Begin to structure your notes around the design of the book. Decide how much material you wish to learn. Draw a picture of the organization of it. Put the more important information to the left, details to the right.

Leave more room under topics and titles that have more pages involved. Draw these maps and lines before reading to help your mind organize and store the data better. After a

THE STUDY PROCESS! (FINDING THE MAIN IDEAS)

Before you read a chapter in depth, first skim through it and pick out the main ideas by noting key "signposts" along the way.

chapter or section, go back and add to your notes. Figure 4 provides an illustration of this method.

2. <u>Ask</u> Questions in Each Assigned Chapter.

Move quickly, skimming through the chapter much faster than your usual reading rate. Your purpose here is to find out what is important and how it is presented, not to read it. Check all boldfaced headings, <u>turning each into a question</u> you will answer later. Copy under the chapter titles, each of the subtitles, and the main ideas. This will take only a few seconds a page, but it will give you important clues to the material and help you to read it faster later on because you will be prepared for new ideas. Look over the visual aids, such as maps, charts, diagrams, illustrations, and pictures. That will help you grasp each point quickly. Then read any summaries or questions included at the end of the chapter. Summaries usually are helpful because they include the points the author felt to be most important.

Before proceeding with your study, set two goals. Set a *comprehension goal*; decide how well you need to know the material. Will you be tested? If so, how thoroughly? Set a *time goal* for your particular section or chapter based upon how well you need to know it. In easy or familiar material, your goal may be fifteen pages an hour. But whatever your goal, make

Figure 4.
A Guide for Preparing to Read

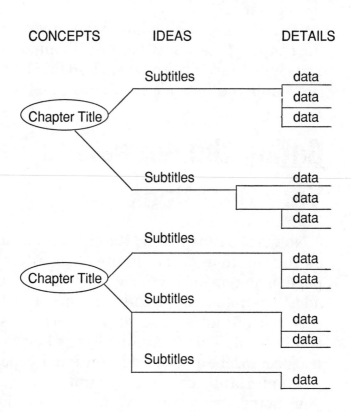

sure that it is only for one chapter or section—setting lengthy or unrealistic goals only leads to discouragement and failure. By achieving both of these goals, you will speed your study time greatly.

At this stage you should have in your notes the chapter title, subtitles, and all major ideas. You should already know a lot about the material—and you haven't even read it yet!

3. <u>Gather</u> the Answers to Your Questions

Now is the time to read the chapter as quickly as you can to understand the ideas. After each page or major idea, go back to your notes and add the supporting details to them. Don't proceed more than a page without writing something down. This is an important key to textbook comprehension and retention. Respond to the material by continually summarizing it in your notes, using your own words. The old way of studying was to read and forget. Get into the habit of reading and responding. You will find even the most boring books become interesting.

Reduce the use of underlining seemingly important thoughts; do not use hi-liter, magic marker, or felt tip pens. Such a study method:
1. is premature; you are not in a position to judge what is most important until you've read the entire chapter.
2. postpones learning; you may simply color

the material, rather than understand it.

3. is permanent; have you ever tried to erase it?
4. gives all material equal weight.
5. distracts; have you tried to read a us book marked with hi-liter?
6. devaluates the book; it ruins the appearance and resale value of the book.

Instead, use a pencil to mark important ideas. Whenever something looks valuable, put a check mark in the margin, just to the side of the passage. It marks what is important, but is not permanent. Later on, during a review, you can re-evaluate your marks and either leave them in place, erase them, or add a second one for emphasis. This system is one of the most valuable tools you can use. Not only is it flexible, but it is quite inexpensive. Continue reading each chapter, marking what is important with a check, and adding to your notes until you are finished.

4. Evaluate Your Results.

Go back through the chapter and reread it quickly to refresh your memory. Answer the chapter questions, see relationships, and complete your notes. Look at your notes. Do you now have details to support each main idea? Can you study that chapter from your notes? The answer should be yes. Your goal has been to get the material out of the text into your notes, then into your mind. Textbooks written by scientists or professors are often wordy and difficult to understand. Put the ideas in your own words and you will learn the material much faster

The following questions can help you evaluate textbooks and other nonfiction works:

1. Do you clearly understand the author's goal? If not, check the preface, foreword, and introduction?

2. Do you understand how the author has presented his material? What do you think is the general method of presentation? What are the main ideas? Minor ones? Check the table of contents for these answers.

3 What are the conclusions drawn by the author? Do you agree with them? Why did the author come to those conclusions? If you do not agree, in what areas was the author weak? Were his premises weak or only his conclusions?

4. How would you compare the author with anyone else you may have read? Is the book up to date? What else have you read that either reaffirmed or conflicted with it? In what ways?

5. Now can you relate the text material to class lecture notes?

Spend time to integrate and remember your material because it is as important as reading it. If your notes are unclear, try rewriting them, basing your organization around the main ideas. Think about the concepts presented in the chapter and try to explain them in your own words. Practice recalling information with and without your notes. Try to study as much as possible from your notes. They are bound to be more understandable than the text. Do not spend your time reading and rereading your texts. Your exams are a test of your thinking and recalling abilities, not usually your reading skills. So practice thinking and recalling your notes and the text material. The study process you have just learned demands proof of your effectiveness through organization and recall. It is simple, yet effective. Let's review the four parts.

REVIEW THESE POINTS

Attack Plan for Studying
1. Prepare for reading by browsing through your texts.
    *   Copy chapter titles.
    *   Structure notes.
2. Ask questions in each assigned chapter.
    *   Add subtitles and main ideas to notes.
    *   Set goals.
3. Gather the answers to your questions.
    *   Use a pencil check system; don't underline.
    *   Add details to notes for each page.
4. Evaluate your results.
    *   Fill gaps in notes where needed.
    *   Answer questions.
    *   Think and recall.

Figure 5.
The Study Process

P-A-G-E

Use these steps for mastery of your subject area.

PREPARE:
Prepare your study environment.
Prepare your materials, supplies, attitude.
Browse through the book, covers, and table of contents.
Check out visual aids, vocabulary, and chapter length.
Begin to map out your notes with key ideas.

ASK QUESTIONS:
In the assigned section, browse more carefully.
Ask key questions; be curious and critical.
Note main ideas, topic sentences, and subtitles.
Study visual aids; locate key points.
Discover what you already know.
Decide what you need to know.
Know in what form you'll need to know it.
Decide on your overall study purpose; set short specific
    goals.

GATHER INFORMATION:
Read to answer questions, not to memorize.
Stay in flow—keep moving.
Note key points, answers to questions.
Mark with a pencil check in margin.
Stop after each page and add details to your notes to
    support the main ideas.
Save complete notetaking for the last step.

EVALUATE:
Add to notes from text.
Complete your understanding—fill gaps.
Review new vocabulary words.
Use mnemonic devices to learn key points.
Use the table of contents or index to review.
Recreate notes from memory as a review tool.
Practice recalling, not rereading.

Figure 6.
Sample Notes* for Chapter 3

*See pages 103–107 for a description of how to prepare creative notes like these.

CHAPTER 4

READING FOR RESULTS:

Speed and Comprehension

Every man who knows how to read has it in his power to magnify himself, to multiply the ways in which he exists, to make his life full, significant, and interesting."

Aldous Huxley

As important as reading is to success in school, many students dislike it. Those who do like to read are usually good at it. A conclusion one might reach is that people like to do things they're good at. This chapter is designed to help you get good at reading so even if you still dislike some of your texts, at least you'll be able to dislike them for less time. This first section is on rapid reading—an essential for success in school.

Most students with poor grades need help in reading skills. Yet, it's no wonder—their last reading lesson was probably in the second grade, and it's unlikely anyone has had a class in comprehension or speed since then. High-powered reading skills can help make school more enjoyable and create plenty of free time. One of the most fascinating areas of learning involves rapid reading skills.

READING FOR SPEED

1. You Can Read Much Faster!

Would it help you if you could read twice as fast as you presently read? How about twenty times as fast, and with better comprehension? If that sounds impossible, it's not. The human mind is capable of seeing and understanding material as fast as one can turn pages, and some people do read that fast. John Stuart Mill,

Teddy Roosevelt, and John F. Kennedy were all naturally fast readers, as have been many others. They were what are known as gifted readers; those who read very fast with excellent comprehension. Gifted readers come from every walk of life, for reading is a skill not related to age, occupation, heredity, or intelligence. The only reason that you may not read fast now is because your natural gifts may have been smothered in school.

The way reading is taught in most public schools is the same technique used a century ago. Curiously, the average American reads at about the same rate today as he read 100 years ago. Most people read between 100 and 400 words per minute, the national average. But slow readers are severely penalized throughout life and are simply unable to keep up because of the tremendous volume of reading required today. Hopefully, schools will change their methods of reading instruction so that someday all students will be rapid readers. In theory, the only things that should decide reading rate are the student's background in the subject, the purpose for reading, and the ability to turn pages. Some readers have been tested in difficult textbook material who have read thousands of words per minute with excellent comprehension. That's over a dozen pages per minute. Yet some of these super-readers used to read at rates near 200 words per minute! So it is certainly possible for the average reader to increase his or her reading speed considerably.

What does limit your reading rate? Poor habits such as subvocalization (pronouncing words to yourself), regression (going back to reread material already covered), prolonged fixation (stopping and staring at one word), and inefficient eye movement (losing your place and wandering between lines). These poor habits cause tired eyes, boredom, low speeds, and low comprehension. It is not ability that you lack, it is training. Because we are taught to read at 100 to 400 words per minute, we are led to believe that is our "normal rate." But those rates are no more normal than 10 or 10,000 words per minute. To improve your rate, it takes proper training and time.

A book cannot give the same kind of help that is necessary to make a dramatic increase in your reading skills. Unfortunately, machine speed-reading courses force faster reading without actually breaking the crippling bad habits. The mechanical pacer used with most speed-reading machines becomes a crutch that cannot be taken into all reading situations. Several courses actually break the habits causing low speeds and poor comprehension, provided you are willing to spend time working at it. Until you can get some professional help from a well-trained rapid-reading instructor, there *are* some positive steps you can take.

2. Read with Your Hand.

As children, we were generally taught not to underline words with our fingertips. But this method actually helps increase speed and comprehension. It builds speed in reading

READ WITH YOUR HAND!

"This method builds speed in reading because it prevents unnecessary backing up and rereading, which consumes about one-sixth of your reading time."

because it prevents unnecessary backing up and rereading, which consumes about one-sixth of your reading time. It also prevents unneeded prolonged fixations, the habit of staring at one word or phrase for a long period. Reading with your hand on the page improves your comprehension because it directs your attention to a spot instead of allowing your eyes and mind to wander. Simply place your fingertip under the first word and move it along at a comfortable rate, underlining each word. Be sure to pick up your finger at the end of each line, lifting it to begin the next one. Read directly above your fingertip and watch your rate soar.

3. Learn to Adjust Your Rates.

Don't read everything at the same rate. You should read light fiction quickly and technical texts at about one-half that rate. When you read easy material, speed up and you will enjoy reading more. A common misconception is that reading faster ruins enjoyment. That is not true. When you were in first grade, you probably read at a rate of 10 to 50 words per minute. Now you may read 100 to 500 words per minute, a full ten times faster! Did you lose any of the enjoyment of books? Of course not, and in fact, you may enjoy books more now than when you read slowly. Decide upon your purpose and read to seek the level of comprehension you require. When your purpose in reading is entertainment, read faster than usual. In a high responsibility situation, take notes often, re-read difficult passages, and read at your maximum rate of comprehension, not to memorize.

4. See Yourself as a Good Reader.

Do you see yourself as a slow reader or as a fast reader? Your actions are consistent with your conception of yourself. Always push yourself, being aware of what you need to get out of the material. Believe you can get what you want, when you want it. Seeing yourself as a fast reader can become a self-fulfilling prophecy.

Dr. Maxwell Maltz, author of *Psycho-Cybernetics*, popularized the concept of mental practice, and thousands have used it successfully. He believes each person has a goal-striving mechanism that simply needs to be triggered properly in order to automatically steer a person toward a set goal. What does this mean to you in practical terms? It means that you can "program" yourself to become a better reader, or anything else you like, by using a beautiful built-in success mechanism. This success mechanism is a goal-directed instinct that is easily motivated.

Make sure the goal you seek is desirable. Otherwise your internal mechanism may not get the clear signal it needs. Get a strong, clear, and vivid picture of yourself achieving the role you wish. If it's reading improvement you wish, sit back, close your eyes, and picture yourself sitting down at a desk or table you know well, moving down the page, not only comprehending what you have read, but quickly recalling it in your notes. Practice this once or twice a day for about two minutes each time. Within several weeks you should see a notable improvement in yourself.

5. See More Words at A Time.

One reason you might read slowly is that you read with a narrow, constricted, "hard focus"; you have disciplined your eyes to see only a couple of words at a time. This severely limits your speed. Your reading focus is different from your usual vision. The difference is easy to explain. What do you see when you look outside your window? Do your eyes focus only on a spot three-quarters of an inch by five-eighths of an inch? What you see is an entire panorama with everything in focus. You should see a page in the same way.

In order to regain your usual range of vision for reading, you will need some practice. This will require the use of both hands and a large book. Flip through the pages of the book quickly, turning them from the top with your left hand and pulling your eyes down the page by brushing down each page with the edge of your right hand. Your fingers should be extended and relaxed. Follow your hand down each page with your eyes, trying to see as many words as possible. Start by brushing each page in two or three seconds, gradually reducing the time spent on each page until you can go as fast as you can turn pages. Pace yourself, starting at twenty pages a minute, slowly increasing to one hundred pages a minute within one to two months. This practice work helps your eyes see more words at a time by preventing zooming in or focusing only on individual words. Practice for five minutes a day for several weeks. Remember that it is unlikely that you'll read faster without practicing. Reading is a skill, and as with any skill, all the instruction in the world won't help you unless you actually practice what you learn. It's important to learn to see more words at a time. Just those few minutes a day of practice will help prevent missing words.

Some students are afraid that if they go faster, they'll miss words. But they already know most of the words they're about to see. There are over 600,000 words in our language, but 400 hundred of them comprise 65 percent of printed material. These are structure words that have no meaning, but they tie the sentence together. For example, in the second sentence of this paragraph, the structure words are: *but, of, the, about, to*. Remove most of those words and the sentence is choppy, but still readable: "they already know most words they're about see." Because you've read those 400 words many times, don't let them slow down your reading by dwelling on them.

A famous psychologist, James Cattell, determined through research that our untrained visual capacity is about four words in one-hundredth of a second. That's 400 words a second or 24,000 words per minute that we're capable of seeing and understanding. Australian psychologist John Ross has reported that the human mind can process depth information in .0002 seconds. He defines depth information as nonfiction technical material. Some students may wonder whether or not they can comprehend material by reading at a faster rate. Accept the fact that you can. Just practice at it and you'll see results immediately.

Don't worry about understanding everything when you read fast. You can see and understand everything, but merely reading something does not insure retention. You'll retain information by practicing recall, not by reading slower. Usually the slower you read, the more the mind wanders, with little comprehension and recall.

The ideal level on which to read is a purely mental or intellectual plane. This means don't clog or block information in your mind by negative emotions such as anxiety, worrying, and fear of "not getting it." If you develop an open, positive, "go-for-it" attitude, you'll read much better.

At higher rates of speed it's also helpful to talk to yourself. Discuss out loud the topic of each paragraph for additional clarity and reinforcement. Conceptual vocalization, the skill of thinking out loud, enables you to better process ideas and concepts.

In order to get the comprehension you need at faster speeds, it helps to have an adequate background in the material. You can get background information from: 1) reading other material on that subject, 2) personal experience, and 3) prereading. The purpose of prereading is to become familiar with the main ideas and to organize those ideas into a pattern. This organizing step is crucial in developing speed in reading textbook material.

One other hint that will help you read fast is often overlooked: hold your book four to six inches *farther* away from your eyes than usual. Your eyes won't have to work so hard because the farther things are from your eyes, the less movement it takes to see them all. So be sure your material is at least fifteen inches from your eyes; you'll enjoy increased speed and comprehension, and reduce fatigue.

READING FOR COMPREHENSION

1. Read Quickly to Improve Concentration.

Readers with the best comprehension are usually fast readers. The slower you read, the more chances there are for you to daydream and lose concentration, hence, comprehension. Getting good comprehension is a process and a habit, not a mystery. Actually, comprehension is a two-fold process: 1) perceiving and organizing information, and 2) relating that information to what you already know. Several factors determine the degree of comprehension you'll get from the material you read. Those factors are your background in that subject, your reading skills and the organization and presentation of that material.

There is virtually no comprehension when the reader does not have the necessary vocabulary and background. Comprehension is largely dependent on how well the reader already knows the subject. Because background increases the vocabulary and subject familiarity, get the most amount of prior knowledge you can. Then processing becomes almost subliminal, it happens so fast. When the reader has an extensive background, there is even a point at which material can be read prior to conscious awareness. Background is the reason why a beginning law student might read at 70 to 200 words per minute, yet a practicing attorney can read the same material much faster. Therefore, the first habit to get into that will build comprehension is to gain the necessary background for that subject. Two excellent ways to accomplish this are listening to lectures and reading other easier material on the same subject.

2. Read Actively for Greater Meaning.

Reading is an active process, not a passive one. Anticipate ideas and read for a purpose to answer your questions by actively searching for the information you want. Have questions in mind before you read, not afterwards. If you begin reading a book with questions, you'll complete your reading with the answers. Think about important points and read to understand them. Be confident that you can get what you want and you will. Don't argue with the author while reading. Save critical analysis for later so you will not slow yourself down, lose concentration, and miss the flow of the material. Put a pencil check in the margin of areas you would like to go back to.

3. Read to Understand, Not to Memorize.

In order to have a smooth, continuous flow of information to your mind, don't stop to memorize facts. Save that process for later when you study your notes. Read a page, summarize the data in your notes, then continue. At all times you should read as rapidly as you can understand the ideas.

4. Maintain Proper Attitude and Desire.

You must care about what you are reading or studying. If you don't, create a need to care. Use positive reinforcement. You might say to yourself, "Once I get this reading done, I'll be able to go do something I enjoy more." Don't use negative reinforcement or a self-threat such as, "If I don't get an *A* in this class, I'll lose my scholarship." If you maintain a strong, receptive attitude, you will find comprehension will be easier because you are not fighting yourself. Fighting reading is much like panicking while swimming. The secret is to relax.

5. Upgrade Poor Physical Habits.

It's difficult to comprehend what you read when you are tired, sleepy, depressed, or in pain. Some students complain that their comprehension is poor while doing their reading at three in the morning. At that hour, many couldn't comprehend the morning newspaper. It is critical not only to be alert, but relaxed. Be comfortable and in tune with the subject of the book. Reading posture definitely affects comprehension. Sit at a desk when possible. Study in an upright position with the book flat on the table, fifteen or more inches away. The more stretched out and relaxed your study position, the more you will encourage its usual result—drowsiness, poor concentration, or sleep. If you want comprehension, speed, and retention, sit up alertly, and act as though you are serious about accomplishing the task.

6. Use the Multilayered Learning Process.

The study procedure described in the previous chapter is an extremely useful tool for comprehension. Basically it involves approaching the material on several levels, and taking notes after each. As a review, here are the steps:

1. Prepare and preview the material, noting boldfaced headings, summaries, subtitles, visual aids, and topic sentences. Map out your notes with key ideas. Browse through the material, becoming aware of its structure, complexity, and organization.
2. Ask questions. Set your purpose—exactly what level of comprehension do you need? How far away is the exam? With your purpose in mind, set a realistic chapter or section goal.
3. Gather your answers. Read the material, a chapter at a time, moving as quickly as you can understand the ideas. Stop after each page and add details to your notes to support the main ideas.
4. Evaluate. Review your notes and text, filling in gaps, viewing the overall content and organization, and refreshing your memory. Think about and recall the information.

7. Organize What You Read.

Your mind seeks organization, logical sequences, and order. Give it a chance to comprehend the material by grouping ideas and details into meaningful blocks. Restructure the material into easy-to-picture thoughts. Use every possible combination of thought-pictures that will work. When you perceive the unity and structure of the material you are studying you will grasp its meaning much faster. Strive toward understanding the structure as well as the details.

8. Write as You Read.

Get in the habit of recalling on paper immediately what you have read. Because you will understand each point better, the following point will be that much clearer. Comprehension depends upon understanding each preceding idea. The better you understand and recall one idea, the more likely you will understand the next. Stick to each part of the study process and you will find comprehension becoming a habit.

REVIEW THESE POINTS

Reading for Speed

1. You can read much faster.
2. Read with your hand.
3. Learn to adjust your rates according to material and purpose.
4. See yourself as a good reader.
5. See more words at a time.

Reading for Comprehension

1. Read quickly to improve concentration.
2. Read actively for greater meaning.
3. Read to understand, not to memorize.
4. Maintain proper attitude and desire.
5. Upgrade poor physical habits.
6. Use the multilayered learning process.
   - Prepare
   - Ask
   - Gather
   - Evaluate
7. Organize what you read.
8. Write as you read.

Figure 7
Sample Notes* for Chapter 4

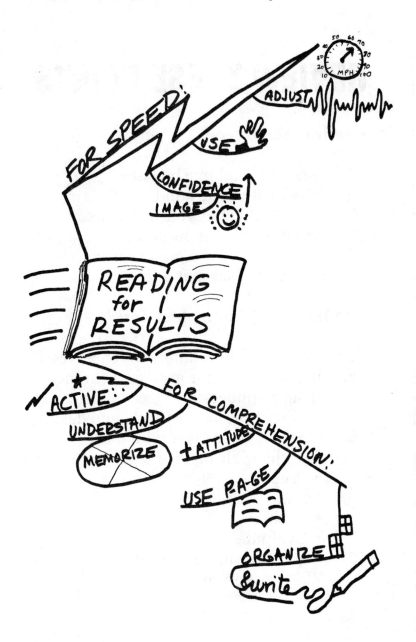

*See pages 103–107 for a description of how to prepare creative notes like these.

CHAPTER 5

NOTES THAT SPARKLE:

The Kind of Notes You'll Love to Study

"First we raise the dust, then we claim, we cannot see."
Berkeley

Efficient notes are vital to straight *A's*. Most of your studying should be done from notes taken in class and from the text. Your notes show how well you understand the material presented. Students are not usually taught how to take concise, creative notes. Most have to learn from others or through trial and error. Learn the following basics for general usage. Then use your creativity to develop some formats that work best for you and the subjects in which you are interested.

NOTETAKING SKILLS

1. Make Sure Your Notes Summarize—Not Duplicate—the Material.

Your notes should not be a recreation, but rather a synopsis, a synthesis. Accuracy is your first consideration. But beyond that, try to reconstruct the material in your own words. That is the beauty of good notes; they are more understandable and interesting than a text or lecture. Include as many examples as time or necessity permits.

Table 1.
Symbols for Use in Notetaking

SYMBOL	EXPLANATION
>	greater than, more than
<	less than
=	the same, equals
≠	not the same, different
X	times, cross, trans
→	towards, going
←	from
∴	therefore, because
∞	infinity, a great deal
(+)	positive, good
(-)	negative, against
$\bar{c}$, w/	with
w/o	without
↓	down, under, decreasing
↑	above, up, increasing
$	dollars, money
Q	question

2. Devise Your Own Shorthand.

It is time-consuming to spell out each word you choose to include in your notes. You can phonetically abbreviate by using the consonants of a word to create a phonetic representation, which you will be able to write rapidly and interpret easily upon review. Look at the following sentence from a lecture given in a literature class:

Jean-Paul Sartre is a French existentialist who was born in Paris in 1905.

Your notes might read as follows:

Sartre, exis, Paris 1905.

Use as many symbols and abbreviations from math as you can. Table 1 shows some symbols that can be used for shortcuts in notetaking.

3. Vary the Size of Titles and Headings.

The thoughts and ideas you record will not all be of the same importance. With some practice, you will begin to automatically write more important ideas in larger size print and details much smaller. Such variations will help you remember your notes more easily, and make them more fun to take down. Another method that is helpful is the use of geometric shapes to identify and categorize ideas. Table 2 shows some examples.

4. Learn the Basic Format of the Subject.

Each subject group has basic characteristics, which help you organize information and your thoughts on that particular subject. Many students are stumped in notetaking because in some textbooks the information on each page is not well organized. Some books may go for a dozen pages without boldfaced headings or changes in organization. Difficulty often occurs in studying and taking notes from such textbooks. Fortunately, most textbooks are better written today than they were years ago. Many have chapter summaries, boldfaced headings, and questions to answer. But when you use a book that does not indicate what is important by its format, use the information in Table 3 to help organize your notes and study procedure. Table 3 includes the basic formats for three main subject areas.

In order to take notes well, you must be proficient at sorting information. To understand an idea, you need to see its parts as well as its whole. Depending on the subject, the parts are quite predictable. First, find the main idea; it is often in the first two sentences of each paragraph. To do that, look for phrases like

Table 2.
Geometric Key for Use in Notetaking

GEOMETRIC SYMBOL	EXPLANATION
☐	Main Ideas: Inserted in square or Marked with check
√ √ √	Important Concepts or Facts to Remeber: Marked with two checks
⬭	Names of People: Circled
▭	Minor Ideas or Details: Inserted in rectangle
△	Reasons, Why, How: Inserted in triangle
⟶ LETTER SIZE	Relationships or Connecting Ideas: Indicated by arrows and letter size to show subordinate ideas

"most important," "first of all," "it must be emphasized that . . . ." Any similar phrase is the author's way of telling you that something important is being said.

Second, find supporting details and examples to explain the main idea and often include stories or data, such as names and dates.

Next, isolate the information you will need by sorting actual facts from filler data such as the author's personal experiences and opinions. This is easy because the facts are often proper names, places, or numbers. Once isolated from the facts, the remaining material can often be identified as filler.

Texts often follow a sequence. For example, math texts might follow this sequence: Background information, statement of laws, axioms, or theorems, examples, problems presented to be solved. When you take notes for a math class, don't simply copy an important theorem. Ensure comprehension by examining the other parts of the sequence of information.

5. Use a Creative Approach, Not the Standard Outline Form.

The more unusual and eye-catching your notes are, the more likely you will enjoy studying them and be able to recall them. Don't use the standard outline form except as a last

Table 3.
Basic Subject Formats for Use in Notetaking

SUBJECT AREA	FORMAT AND STRUCTURE
Social Sciences Law Political Science History Sociology Psychology	Issues and principles Background information Problems, conflicts Reasoning, procedure Decisions, results Conclusions, alternatives

Exact Sciences
Math
Biology
Physics
Chemistry
	Background, idea
	   description
	Laws, theorems, axioms
	Supportive examples,
	   approach
	New problems to solve
	Solutions, other applications

Literature Novels Plays Poetry	Background on author, topic Characters Problems, issues defined Events, complications Crises, problem solved

resort. Its two major drawbacks are inflexibility and difficulty in recalling. Helpful, creative notes take very little practice, but if you need some ideas, refer to Figures 8-14.

The whole idea is to make your notes more brain compatible. That means designing your notes more like the way your brain stores information instead of the traditional outline method. Your recall of individual words generally is low. However, your brain stores information as pictures, sounds, and feelings *very* well. That means, put as much sensory information as possible into your notes and they'll work better for you.

Start by thinking of your notes as a creative pattern of connected ideas. Make them similar to a sentence diagram, road map, blueprint, recall pattern, or schematic clustering instead of a list. The purpose of this format is for clarity and recall. At best, your notes may generate refreshing ideas, great recall, and more creativity. At a minimum, they'll store information and be relaxing and fun. You might use these creative notes for lectures, organizing your thoughts, or study notes.

The method to great notes is simple. Get colored pens and start in the middle of the paper, then: 1) decide on a main topic or idea; 2) print the topic in the center of your paper and enclose it; 3) add branches to hold the important points; 4) add details and key words on to the branches; 5) add symbols and pictures for better recall.

In textbooks, articles, and other nonfiction, the branches could be titled from the boldfaced

BE CREATIVE IN YOUR NOTES!

"The more unusual and eye-catching your notes are, the more likely you will enjoy studying them."

print or chapter headings, or simply labelled what, how, why, who, and when. If there are no clues, make up labels such as purpose, methods, and result. In fiction, use branch labels such as chapter titles, character names, places, events, problems, or conclusions. Then attach the details to those branches.

Additional tips: Use pictures, arrows, symbols, cartoons, illustrations, and abbreviations. Put your words on the top of lines; be brief and simple. Turn the paper sideways and use medium to thick colored pens. Printing is more easily recalled than script. Change the size of your words; the more important they are, the bigger they might be made. Use a different color for each of the branches. Be outrageous! Put in action, creativity, and your own personality. At the end of most chapters of this book, I have given you samples. The only element missing, and it's an important one, is color.

6. Keep Class Lecture Notes and Text Study Notes Together.

An ingenious way to learn a subject quickly and with better understanding is to take notes in tandem. Take class lecture notes on a page opposite the notes you took while studying the text.

Ideally, you should read the text and take notes prior to the class lecture. Put your notes on the left-hand side of your paper, leaving the right half for class work (See Figure 13). Then when the professor lectures, you will not only understand his comments better, but you won't have to write as much (See Table 4). If you keep class and text notes on the same topic together on a page, you will take fewer notes and understand more. Other students in class may be writing frantically while you relax and only jot down an occasional supporting detail. Even if you can't take text notes in advance, bring your lecture notes home and reverse the process.

7. Recreate Your Notes.

The last step in notetaking is the most important one. Once you have completed your notes for class, test yourself. Either your notes worked for you or they didn't. The way you test yourself is simple: pull out a blank piece of paper and recreate your notes from memory.

If you're able to recreate 80 to 90 percent or better, congratulations. If it's anything less than that, you need to make some changes in the way you take notes. That means you must create a more brain compatible format, maybe something that meets your own personal learning style better. Here are some suggestions:
- Use more pictures and illustrations.
- Print instead of writing in script.
- Color code your key ideas—one color per idea.
- Organize the material differently.

- Use less detail.
- Use more diversity of print size and caps.

There's only one reason you're taking notes: to learn the material. If you're learning it, great. If not, change what you're doing. Notetaking can be a lot of fun *if* it's done creatively, *if* you test its effectiveness before the test, and *when* it pays off for you at test time.

REVIEW THESE POINTS

Notetaking skills

1. Make sure your notes summarize, not duplicate, the material.
2. Devise your own shorthand.
3. Vary the size of titles and headings.
4. Learn the basic format of the subject.
5. Use a creative approach, not the standard outline form.
6. Keep class lecture notes and text study notes together.
7. Recreate your notes to test yourself.

Figure 8
Sample Notes* for Chapter 5

*See pages 103–107 for a description of how to prepare creative notes like these.

Figure 9.
Sample Notes for Chemistry

These notes, based on the format for exact sciences, include subject description, laws, examples, problems to solve, and solutions. Here is a sample:

Notes, p. 114

Activation Energy
    amt. needed to change
    from pot. to kin. energy
    see $\longrightarrow$

activation energy

energy released

(+)

(0)

(—)

Heat of Reaction
    application to chem.
    problems—only 2 of 3
    sources needed $\longrightarrow$

$$CO + NO_2 \longleftrightarrow CO_2 + NO$$
if $NO_2 = 32$
$CO_2 = 86$
then ...... $32 = 86 + (-54)$
$\therefore \Delta H = (-54)$

Catalysts
    no chem. change. speeds
    reac. + more E per reac.
    as H + ions in

$$HCOOH \longleftrightarrow HO_2 + CO$$

Figure 10.
Sample Notes for Law Texts

This format helps to organize a law case quickly and clearly. While a third year law student would look for a different approach from that of a first-year student, the basic information is the same.

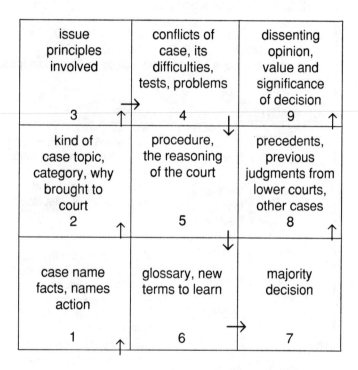

Figure 11A
Sample Notes for Novels: Type A

This format includes background on author, characters, settings, problems, events, crises, and solutions.

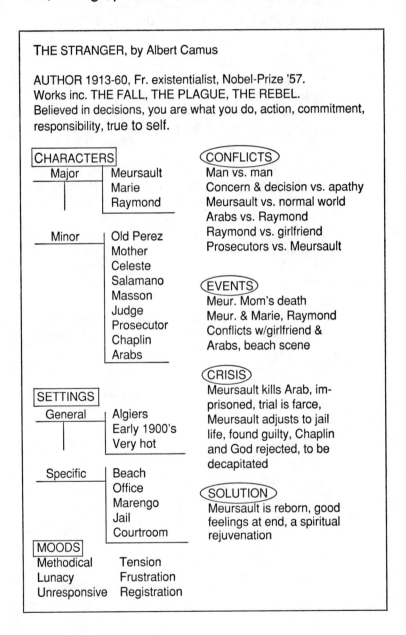

THE STRANGER, by Albert Camus

AUTHOR 1913-60, Fr. existentialist, Nobel-Prize '57.
Works inc. THE FALL, THE PLAGUE, THE REBEL.
Believed in decisions, you are what you do, action, commitment, responsibility, true to self.

CHARACTERS
Major
- Meursault
- Marie
- Raymond

Minor
- Old Perez
- Mother
- Celeste
- Salamano
- Masson
- Judge
- Prosecutor
- Chaplin
- Arabs

SETTINGS
General
- Algiers
- Early 1900's
- Very hot

Specific
- Beach
- Office
- Marengo
- Jail
- Courtroom

MOODS
Methodical   Tension
Lunacy   Frustration
Unresponsive Registration

CONFLICTS
Man vs. man
Concern & decision vs. apathy
Meursault vs. normal world
Arabs vs. Raymond
Raymond vs. girlfriend
Prosecutors vs. Meursault

EVENTS
Meur. Mom's death
Meur. & Marie, Raymond
Conflicts w/girlfriend &
Arabs, beach scene

CRISIS
Meursault kills Arab, imprisoned, trial is farce, Meursault adjusts to jail life, found guilty, Chaplin and God rejected, to be decapitated

SOLUTION
Meursault is reborn, good feelings at end, a spiritual rejuvenation

Figure 12.
Sample Notes for History

Catergorize your information so that you will follow the flow of events better. This format allows a better understanding of details as well as major events.

THE CIVIL WAR

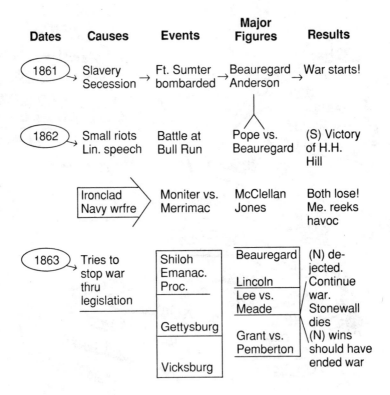

Figure 13.
Sample Notes for Philosophy

In these notes, the left-hand side was prepared in advance, from the texts. Then the page of notes is taken to the class lecture so that traditional comments can be made on the right-hand side.

Aristotle's Critique of Spartan Constitution

BACKGROUND ON ARTIST
    Current society is ?
    Scien-philos-astron-
    "A is A," concretes,
    the realistic, specifics
 	
A's ANALYSIS OF S.C.
    (−) pop. mngmnt.
    (−) laws
        property laws
    bribes $
    no election of ovrsrs
    (-) treasury low on $
    (+) excess lifetime offcrs
    (+) must add soldiers
 	
(Q's FOR CLASS)
    implications of his crit.
    justified?
    Compr/contr w/US
        Constit.
    define "polis"
            "Ephoralty"	

Figure 14.
Sample Text Notes

These notes show the use of a variety of techniques useful in taking brief, well-organized notes from a textbook.

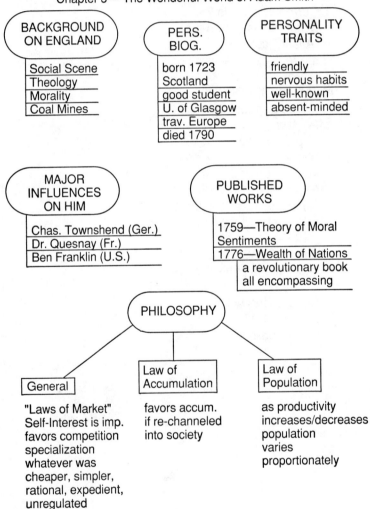

THE WORLDLY PHILOSPOHER
by Robert Heibroner
Chapter 3—"The Wonderful World of Adam Smith"

BACKGROUND ON ENGLAND
Social Scene
Theology
Morality
Coal Mines

PERS. BIOG.
born 1723
Scotland
good student
U. of Glasgow
trav. Europe
died 1790

PERSONALITY TRAITS
friendly
nervous habits
well-known
absent-minded

MAJOR INFLUENCES ON HIM
Chas. Townshend (Ger.)
Dr. Quesnay (Fr.)
Ben Franklin (U.S.)

PUBLISHED WORKS
1759—Theory of Moral Sentiments
1776—Wealth of Nations
a revolutionary book
all encompassing

PHILOSOPHY

General
"Laws of Market"
Self-Interest is imp.
favors competition
specialization
whatever was
cheaper, simpler,
rational, expedient,
unregulated

Law of Accumulation
favors accum.
if re-channeled
into society

Law of Population
as productivity
increases/decreases
population
varies
proportionately

Table 4.
Lecture Notetaking Responsibilities

Responsibility	Objective	Procedure
Listen	Anticipate your purpose.	Decide if you need to remember everything in the lecture or only main ideas. Determine what material you will be responsible for on a test. Determine if the lecture is a complement to your reading assignment or new material.
	Spend most of your time listening, not taking notes.	Listen to understand. Listen for entire ideas. Summarize ideas. Determine the main points. Decide how the main points are being made
	Think and concentrate as you listen.	Note examples given. Decide if you agree with the main points. Determine if your previous knowledge allows you to interpret the information differently from the presentation. Try to recall the lecture so that you could present the information covered to someone else.
Take Notes	Be brief.	Write main ideas first. Write details if time allows.
	Use key words.	Write down key words that will allow recall of additional information presented.
	Use symbols.	Take notes using symbols, underlining pictures, cartoons, and arrows.
	Have extra supplies.	Carry spare pens, pencils, and paper.
	Review and reorganize.	Go over notes, rewrite or add extra information while they are fresh in your mind.

CHAPTER 6

USING YOUR MEMORY MORE EFFECTIVELY:

Drawing Mental Pictures

"I'll never forget what's his name."

Norman Pliscou

Harry Lorayne, a well-known memory whiz, once memorized the first 300 pages of the Manhattan telephone directory. Although this feat included over 30,000 names and numbers, he is the first to admit it's not difficult! Memory is an abstraction or process, not an organ. So when we say someone has a good memory, what we really mean is that they are good at memory skills. The activity or skill of remembering can be improved in the same way the skill at chess or tennis can. This is good news! You are not stuck with a poor memory. The reasons that cause poor memory skills can be identified, and steps can be taken to improve memory.

WHY WE FORGET

1. Negative Thinking.

Many of us reinforce our lack of recall so often it makes it difficult to remember. For example, how often have you heard, "I'm awful with names," or "I can never remember numbers"? All this habit does is to encourage the mind not to even try to remember. After all, the excuse has already been given for failure. Don't downplay any part of your memory. It only encourages mental blocks. The first step in improving memory is to believe you can, and eliminate negative thoughts about your ability to do so.

2. A Weak Impression.

It's very easy to forget something that never made a strong impression on you to begin with. This could stem from one or more of the following:
1. Not paying attention to the idea.
2. Not thinking the idea was important.
3. Not having or taking the time to learn the idea.

3. Disuse.

Much like a muscle in the body, you must use your memory in order for it to function at its best. German psychologist Hermann Ebbinghaus studied memory skills and discovered some remarkable statistics. He found that on the average, we forget 70 percent of what we've learned in one hour, and we forget a whopping 84 percent within 48 hours. These figures are based on no usage of memory after initial learning. You can see that disuse of memory is devastating.

4. Interference.

A poor learning situation during a memory activity or static and confusing situations afterwards can cause memory interference. For example, it is not a good idea to try to study geometry immediately after algebra. Your memory will be confused by similar figures and symbols. Accordingly, it would be difficult to memorize a Shakespeare play followed by Dryden's poetry. It's also more difficult to remember things when followed by a period of excitement or emotional intensity. For example, it is not recommended that you go straight from studying history to a homecoming football game. Your mind would experience too much interference for easy recall.

5. Lack of Training

Most people complain about their memories. Yet that seems pretty understandable when you consider that less than 1 percent of all schools offer a class in memory for their students. Because it's unlikely that you were taught much about memory, mistakes are likely to be made out of ignorance.

For example, did you know that your brain has the capacity for one time learning, with no repetition needed? It's true. Did you know that your brain stores information with just three primary senses? They are sight, sound, and feeling. Of course we *do* remember tastes and smells, but a very small part of our brain is used for those two senses compared with, for example, the visual sense. Did you know the amino acid tryptophan has been linked to memory enhancement because of it's role as a neurotransmitter? It's true. Take yourself on a journey—go find a new book in the library about the brain and learn about yourself: how you think and how you remember.

STEPS TO BETTER RECALL

1. Pay Attention.

Being aware is the first step to developing better recall. Begin to notice the part of the page on which information is located. Notice how it's presented and take an extra look at visual aids. Surprisingly, many people do not even know such basic things as what color their walls and curtains are, what their license plate number is, or even their social security number. Knowing these things may not be very important, but learning to be more aware of your surroundings can be very helpful in developing memory skills.

2. Get the Information Right.

Make sure that you correctly understand the data. This sounds like a simple rule, but particularly in the case of remembering statistics, people rarely focus on the numbers themselves. They pay attention to the significance of them. At gatherings where new people are introduced, make sure you understand the name and its spelling. Then repeat it for clarification and reinforcement.

GET THE INFORMATION *RIGHT!*

Make a point of repeating new names for clarification and reinforcement; that way you won't forget them as easily.

3. Tell Yourself You Can.

Telling yourself you can remember is part of developing a healthy self-image. Faith in yourself relaxes and encourages stronger mental processes by opening previously closed thought channels. We can do only what we believe we can.

4. Develop Desire.

Most of the time, the incentive to remember information is already there. But every object of memory is made much stronger when you intensify your desire to recall. If you met someone at a party who interested you, your desire to remember the right name and phone number would be strong. Similarly, when you know you'll be tested on a book, your efforts increase appreciably.

5. Understand.

Though it may sound obvious, make sure you understand thoroughly what you want to remember. This rule applies equally to poetry, mathematics, history, sciences, and related fields. If something makes sense, it's much easier to recall.

6. Be Creative.

One of the most powerful ways to recall is to unleash your imagination. Turn your text material into pictures, change names into pictures, exaggerate, and be artistic. Try to put some color into the data, associating it with sight, sound, taste, and smell.

7. Use Repetition.

Right after a learning activity—within ten minutes and again within 48 hours—refresh your memory through a review. We use both a long-term and a short-term memory and most of what we take in goes into our short-term memory. For example, when you look up a number in the phone book, you remember it just long enough to dial it. Then you promptly forget it. That's, of course, short-term. To get data transferred to our long-term recall, we need to repeat it and use it for reinforcement. The ideal way to study and memorize is to spend six one-hour sessions on a subject, rather than six straight hours. In this way data is reinforced sufficiently to be put into our long-term memory.

8. Create Mental Pictures.

Often called the key to memorizing, mental pictures enable your mind to work in its more

USING MENTAL PICTURES

1. PICTURE A TABLE.
2. IMAGINE IT DANCING.
3. DANCING WITH A HUGE DUCK.
4. WALNUTS ARE RAINING ON THE DUCK.
5. A WALNUT IS CAUGHT BETWEEN YOUR TOES.
6. ON YOUR TOES, YOU SEE A MIRROR INSTEAD of A TOENAIL.
7. IN THE MIRROR, YOU SEE A BEAR.
8. THE BEAR IS IN A CANOE.
9. THE CANOE IS ATTACHED TO A NECKLACE.
10. THE NECKLACE CATCHES ON FIRE.

"Your memory skills will improve if you practice creating mental pictures about what you want to recall. The more unusual and absurd the mental picture you create, the more likely you will be able to recall the word or information associated with it."

natural state. Usually, your mind stores images and pictures, not words. When you think of milk, do you picture the four letters *m-i-l-k*? Most people picture a glass or carton of milk. By the normal storage system, by creating mental pictures, you can remember data much more easily. Change words and ideas into pictures and simply study the pictures, not the words. There are several books in the bibliography on memory and mental pictures that are helpful. Many of these even show how to turn numbers and equations into pictures.

Here's another way to improve your memory with pictures. Did you know that you can use your brain like a TV set to build your recall of any item? You can. You simply need to think of the item, then enhance it the same way you would enhance a video in the production studio. Make the colors stronger, sharpen the focus, make the image bigger and brighter, add a favorite confidence-building sound track and put in your favorite feelings. As you add those components, you'll discover that you suddenly have a better memory of that item.

9. Learn the Technique of Association.

Probably the simplest method of remembering is by association, the process of recalling one item because another reminded you of it. This system requires no more than some awareness and a quick mental picture. For example, if you wanted to remember to bring a pen to class, simply imagine black, gooey ink all over the doorknob where you live. Make a quick but strong mental picture of it. Then when you leave for class, reaching for the doorknob will trigger the mental picture of ink, and you'll remember your pen.

10. Practice Recall Under All Conditions.

If you practice recalling only under "prime" conditions, information may elude you during test time. When you have critical information to remember, create flash cards on 3 × 5-inch index cards to take with you. Then whenever you have a break, at mealtime, while relaxing, or in the library, study the cards and practice recalling.

11. Study Contrasting Subjects.

Apparently our subconscious needs time to sort and categorize information for long-term storage and retrieval. To facilitate this process, do not study two similar subjects back-to-back. Instead, work on a dissimilar subject in between. For example, do not follow the study of algebra with calculus, or Spanish with Italian.

12. Reduce Interference.

Cut down on distractions that might ordinarily follow a study session. It is best to study before a restful, quiet time or even before bed. Then your mind will have time to relax, sort, and store the necessary information.

13. Study Wholes, Not Parts.

Whether the subject is a Shakespearean play or an assignment in anatomy, our mind functions best with complete pictures to remember. Even if you have to memorize only one part of a chapter, become familiar with all of it. For example, if you had to explain to someone why a local beach has low and high tides, it would be much easier if you also discussed how our tides are simply opposite those on the other side of the world. For some reason our recall even varies within the whole picture we are learning. Use the B.E.M. concept for better recall also. We remember material best from the beginning, second best from the end, and our recall is weakest on the middle. Therefore spend more time on the middle to allow for that tendency.

14. Practice Using the Material.

Frequently review, repeat, recite, and use the material you wish to remember. Almost any

PRACTICE RECALL UNDER
ALL
CONDITIONS!

**". . . whenever you have
a break, at mealtime,
while relaxing, or in
the library"**

information learned becomes familiar, and even second nature, through usage. Try to integrate the data into daily usage. There is no substitute for practice.

PRACTICING MENTAL PICTURES

Learn to link one word to another in order to form associations. Your memory skills will improve if you practice creating mental pictures about what you want to recall. The more unusual and absurd the mental picture you create, the more likely you will be able to recall the word or information associated with it.

Use the following ideas to create vivid mental pictures:
1. Imagine some kind of *action* taking place.
2. Form an image that is *out of proportion*.
3. Create in your mind an *exaggerated version* of the subject.
4. Substitute and *reverse* a normal role.
   For example, in order to remember to mail a letter, imagine the letter carrying *you* out to the mailbox and stuffing *you* inside.

Improve your memory skills by practicing word associations using mental pictures. For example, in associating the words *table* and *dance*, first form a clear picture of a table in your mind. Visualize a table that you use frequently, one that is familiar to you. In order to associate *table* with *dance*, imagine the table standing up on two legs, dancing wildly, with the other two legs spinning in the air. Because it is such an absurd picture, it will stick in your mind. Each time you think of table, you will think of dance.

Linking of words can continue in a similar manner. If you wished to next link the word *dance* to *duck*, for example, you might create a mental picture of a huge, six-foot-tall, all white, overfed, potbellied duck dancing and whirling, with feathers flying.

By using the method of linking through mental pictures, you have created a chain of associations: *table* to *dance, dance* to *duck*. In this way, you never try to memorize more than one word at a time. The process is all done with mental pictures. The system of forming associations by using the link method will help you to memorize lists of names, places, events, items, or almost anything. Table 5 includes additional ideas on how to use association.

Table 5.
Forming Associations Between Random Words

Item	Think of	Then associate
table	an enormous table, or a particular table, such as your kitchen table	
dance	imagine a dance	imagine the table dancing, up on two legs
duck	an enormous, overstuffed, six-foot-tall duck, white with orange feet and bill	imagine the duck doing this wild dance
walnuts	millions of walnuts falling out of the sky	imagine the walnuts between the toes
toes	your own toes	imagine huge walnuts between your toes
mirror	very small mirrors the size of a stamp	picture mirrors on the toes instead of toenails
bear	picture a huge brown bear, with your clothes on	imagine the bear seeing himself in the mirror
canoe	picture a dugout canoe	picture the bear paddling around in a canoe
necklace	an enormous, long one	imagine the necklace draped around the canoe
fire	crackling and extra hot	imagine the necklace so hot it's on fire— remove it!

REVIEW THESE POINTS

Why We Forget

1. Negative thinking.
2. A weak impression.
3. Disuse.
4. Interference.
5. Lack of training.

Steps to Better Recall

1. Pay attention.
2. Get the information right.
3. Tell yourself you can.
4. Develop desire.
5. Understand.
6. Be creative.
7. Use repetition.
8. Create mental pictures.
9. Learn the technique of association.
10. Practice recall under all conditions.
11. Study contrasting subjects.
12. Reduce interference.
13. Study wholes not just parts.
14. Practice using the material.

Figure 15.
Sample Notes* for Chapter 6

*See pages 103–107 for a description of how to prepare creative notes like these.

CHAPTER 7

WORD POWER:

Vocabulary and Spelling

"Words are the ammunition of the mind."
Bill Ballance

If you think a good vocabulary would help you get straight *A's*, you are right. In nearly every field, the successful person also has a powerful vocabulary. Scholars believe a good vocabulary is so important that it is a major part of any IQ test. Students with an effective vocabulary excel not only in English, but also in math, science, and business. And the reason they excel is not because they are any smarter, but because they can better express themselves. In almost any business in the country, the higher an employee's position, the better his working vocabulary. Yet, how can you improve your vocabulary?

1. Become Well Read.

Many periodicals are written for people with a sixth-grade education. In order to improve your vocabulary, subscribe to newspapers and magazines of high journalistic quality. Some excellent publications are *Harpers, The Nation, Atlantic Monthly, New Republic, National Review, Commentary, Scientific American, Psychology Today*, and *The New Yorker*. Reading material of this caliber will help you learn many new words.

READ, READ, READ, READ!

"The true master of words goes to the library often."

---

2. Develop Interest in New Words

Use the dictionary to learn new or unfamiliar words. Jot down definitions on a notepad that you keep posted. Refer to it often to refresh your memory. Use new words as often as possible, even to the point of overuse. Try to learn a new word each week. You will be amazed at how quickly your vocabulary increases. The only valid way to add new words to your daily vocabulary is by consciously interjecting them in conversation until you feel comfortable using them.

3. Associate with People Who Have Good Vocabularies.

Expressive, articulate speakers have a way of influencing others. Their ability to express themselves will encourage your use of new words. Your level of communication varies with the people with whom you converse. A college graduate has to simplify language in order to explain to a first grader how a president is elected. But the same person may actually use more difficult and specialized terminology when talking to a professor at school. Associating with people who have a good command of the English language will help to improve your vocabulary and your communication skills.

4. Take a Latin or Greek Class.

The English language evolved from many languages, but a large percentage of the words in our dictionary have a Latin or Greek origin. At a high school, college, or community adult education program, you can enroll in a class that gives a superlative background to word origins and definitions. You may be surprised how much this helps.

5. Get in the Dictionary and Thesaurus Habit.

Whenever you come across a word that is unfamiliar to you or that you don't understand, turn to the dictionary. It is the good speller who uses the dictionary, not the poor one. Get in the habit of referring to the dictionary, regardless of whether you are reading a newspaper or a scholarly journal. The most important thing to remember when looking up definitions of new words is not to stop there. Make use of new words in your daily conversation every chance you get.

A thesaurus is another useful book for learning the meanings of words. A thesaurus is a dictionary of synonyms. For each entry in a thesaurus, many words that have the same or similar meanings are listed. For example, *Roget's Thesaurus* lists 29 synonyms for the word expert, including master, medalist, genius, mastermind, prodigy, first fiddle, and connoisseur. A thesaurus is more complete in its definitions and a lot of fun to use. Browse through one, and you may find words much more interesting.

6. Improve Your Spelling.

Start noticing how words are spelled when you read. Take a course in grammar or composition. Respond to class feedback; when your papers are returned to you, notice the spelling corrections. Sometimes it helps to have another person review your assignments. Pay attention to phonetic sounds, and listen carefully to how words are pronounced. A large percentage of the words in our language are spelled just the way they sound.

Three good ways to sharpen your spelling ability are to learn roots, suffixes, and prefixes. Root words build both spelling and comprehension skills. Table 6 lists ten common roots. Learning them will instantly bring understanding of hundreds of words to your fingertips. Some of the most commonly misspelled, misused words appear in Table 7. Study the table to avoid confusing words that are spelled similarly or pronouced the same.

Table 6.
Common Word Roots

Root	Meaning	Usage
co/com/con	with, together	collaborate, combine, conjugal

bi
  (also tri,
    quad, etc.)
	two, dual	bicycle, bipartisan, bicentennial

chron	time	chronology, chronicle, anachronism
gen	class, race, kind	gender, genre, genius, general
auto	self	automatic, autograph, autonomy, author
trans	across	transfer, transmit, transportation
gram/graph	write	epigram, telegram, graph, stenography,
sub	under	submerge, submit, submarine
super, sur	above	supervise, superfluous, surpass, surtax
dic, dict	say	abdicate, diction, verdict
mal	bad	malevolent, dismal, malefactor
pro	before, forward, in favor of	proponent, propensity, proclivity
ab	from, away from	abduct, abstract, abnormal
dif/dis	not, apart	discord, disparity, differ
circum	around	circumnavigate, circumspect, circumference

Table 7.
Common Errors in Spelling and Usage

Word	Meaning	Usage
then than	shows time compares	**Then** he went home. He is taller **than** I am.
weather whether	relating to climate involves decision	We had nice **weather** today. I don't know **whether** it's right.
accept except	to receive to exclude	Will he **accept** the gift? Everyone laughed **except** Bob.
lose loose	opposite of to find not tight	I did not **lose** it. The belt was **loose**.
already all ready	previously prepared	It's **already** dinner time. She was **all ready**.
its it's	shows possession means it is	The dog wagged **its** tail. **It's** going to be hot.
they're there their	means they are usually shows location or opens a sentence shows possession	**They're** not at home. Sit over **there**. **Their** house.
like	do not use when you really mean "for example"	WRONG: My father is an awful driver. Like last week . . . RIGHT: My father is an awful driver. For example, last week . . .
altogether all together	entirely all in the same place	It's **altogether** too soon. We're **all together** now.

Table 7.
Common Errors in Spelling and Usage
(continued)

Word	Meaning	Usage
break brake	to fracture, shatter, or ruin a stopping device	Don't **break** my heart. Set the parking **brake**.
adapt	to adjust, make suitable, remodel	As much as we may dislike the thought of it, we **adapt** to change quite easily.
adopt	to accept formally, take as one's own	After considerable discussion, the new bylaws were **adopted** by our association.
beside	at the side of	Walking **beside** his mother, he felt safe and content.
besides	in addition to, moreover	**Besides** an obsession for chocolates, I have a weakness for pecans as well.
stationary	fixed, standing still	The shadow of the tree remained **stationary** throughout the hot, breezeless afternoon.
stationery	writing supplies, writing paper	Hoping it would help his case, she had the letter typed on school **stationery**.
principal	most important	The **principal** purpose of the meeting was explained as soon as everyone had quieted down.
principle	basic belief or truth	Such **principles** of human nature as curiosity and greed do not show mankind

REVIEW THESE POINTS

Word Power

1. Become well read.
2. Develop interest in new words.
3. Associate with people who have good vocabularies.
4. Take a Latin or Greek class.
5. Get in the dictionary and thesaurus habit.
6. Improve your spelling.

Figure 16.
Sample Notes* for Chapter 7

*See pages 103–107 for a description of how to prepare creative notes like these.

CHAPTER 8

EVALUATING LITERATURE:

Be an Instant Critic

---

*"Daring as it is to investigate the unknown,
even more so is it to question the known."*

Kaspar

Students are often asked to evaluate books in school. But the skills necessary for assessing a work of fiction usually are not taught in most schools. The many levels of meaning of novels, plays, and poems don't have to elude all but the sharpest students. All it takes is a method of approach, and your desire to follow it through.

HOW TO EVALUATE FICTION

1. Prepare for Reading.

Get together your fiction work and notepaper, and prepare to write. Before you start reading, look at the front and back covers, the preface, and foreword. Then browse through the book to learn the following:

1. How the book is structured—length of chapters, parts, or acts.
2. Who the characters are and where the story takes place (proper names and nouns will be easy to spot, so write them down).
3. How the title is related to the story.

You should have a few notes on the story before you begin reading.

2. Meet the Author.

Every fiction work is an interpretation of some aspect of life as seen through the eyes of the author. Get to know that person and you'll

MEET THE
AUTHOR . . .

"**Get to know the author
and you'll gain insight
into what he or she
writes about and why.**"

gain insight into what he or she writes about and why. The four best ways to meet an author are:

1. Ask your instructor for information on the author's life.
2. Read other books by the same author.
3. Check the book's jacket, introduction, preface, or publisher's notes.
4. Find a biography or autobiography of the author and learn as much as you can.

3.   Organize the Information.

Comprehension and meaning come quickly when the story has unity and flows well. Try to discover the flow of ideas by organizing the information you have recorded into categories. Use the format illustrated in Figure 17 to organize your notes about characters, setting, moods, conflicts, events, complications, crises, and solutions.

The list of characters should include a comment about each of the major ones and a listing of the minor ones. Usually there is one general setting, and many more specific ones, so list them in sequence. For moods, write down how the characters feel about their positions in the action of the story, as well as how you react to each character. Is it light fiction, a horror story, a mystery, or a satire?

To analyze events, crises, and solutions, record happenings of importance in the plot, and the events that led to the crisis or turning point, when things have gone about as far as they can

Figure 17.
Possible Format for Organizing Notes on Fiction

JONATHAN LIVINGSTON SEAGULL

MAIN CHARACTERS
Jonathan
Fletcher
Chiang (Elder)
Sullivan

CONFLICTS / PROBLEMS
Jon vs. friends
Conformity vs. individualism
limits vs. freedom

MINOR CHARACTERS
Judi-Lee
Charles Roland
Jon's Parents

EVENTS
Jon practices flying
perfects speed, maneuvers
Meets Chiang
Goes to Heaven
Jon develops new friends
Fletcher trained as teacher
Jon leaves

SETTINGS
sky
waterfront
heaven

go. Suddenly, the pressure is released, and momentum switches. A major decision is reached, the crisis is resolved, and the remainder of the story is usually a winding down. Sometimes the author's solutions and viewpoints are presented in these last pages of the novel. By organizing your information around these elements of the plot the different levels of meaning will surface quickly, and your understanding of the novel will increase.

4. Ask Questions Before and After Reading.

The questions that follow are designed to help you understand what the author is saying, how he or she says it, and why. They are fairly easy to answer if you review the list before you do your reading. Your mind then will be more alert, subconsciously seeking the answers to each question. Most students gather enough information to evaluate fiction; they just need a way to derive qualitative, meaningful data from it.

Use the following questions to help you evaluate fiction:

What is the author's goal? Why did he or she write the book (to inform, persuade, entertain? Did the author successfully meet this goal? How did the book affect you? Could it have been more effective? What kinds of conflicts are presented? Conflicts include man *vs.* man, man *vs.* nature, and man *vs.* himself. Are they solved? How? How do you feel about the solution? Is it realistic?

Who was the main character in the novel? Does the main character represent the viewpoint of the author? What does the main character believe in? How do you feel about the main character? Why? How does the character meet his or her goals, or are these goals met?

Toward which characters does the author seem to feel most sympathetic and why? Do they represent a political, social, economic, or moral viewpoint? Which one? Are the characters convincing in their role? Were they believable, or supposed to be believable?

What changes do the characters go through in the book? Did they change for the better or for the worse? What caused the change? What do the changes represent?

On what does the author base the book? A historical solution or changing social trend? A recent disaster, politics, or inventions? How does this book fit into literature in general, or current history perspective? Could it have been written more smoothly? Did the book have impact? Would you recommend it to others?

5. Learn Ways to Evaluate an Author's Work.

The more you read, the better equipped you will be to analyze and critique fiction. If you want to critique Hemingway's *A Farewell to*

Arms, there are several approaches you might choose. You might decide to compare it with his other major works. For example, you might read *The Sun Also Rises* and contrast it to *A Farewell to Arms*. To be able to judge Hemingway's style, you might decide to study a variety of writing styles as typified by such American authors as Fitzgerald, Faulkner, Mailer, or Vonnegut.

Examine the author's objective. Is the author trying to inform, entertain, persuade, criticize, or merely sell books? Did the author succeed? Was the dialogue meant to be realistic, and is it? What is the tone of the novel—sarcastic, hopeful, despairing? Is it effective? How long does the author spend on crucial sequences of events as compared with minor events?

Analyze the characters. How are they introduced. Are any introduced and then forgotten? Why? Are the characters consistent in their behavior, or were they meant to be otherwise? Do the conversations fit each character's portrayal? Or do they contradict it? Which character does the author favor and why?

Determine the author's writing style and mechanics. Are any parts of the books so wordy that the plot suffers? Is all of the narration necessary? Is the sentence structure varied? How does the author balance main ideas with minor ones? Does the author keep you interested by creating a desire to continue reading? Do you react the way the characters do? Are you swept into the action? Does the book have a single unifying direction or theme?

Ascertain the author's viewpoint. What philosophies does the author seem to put forth? Does the book reflect the beliefs of Plato, Aristotle, existentialism, realism, or naturalism? At any point is the author illogical, misinformed, prejudiced, incomplete, incorrect, or inconsistent? How do the author's ideas fit into today's thinking? Is the story believable? Was it meant to be? Does the title fit the story?

There is practically an endless list of criteria by which you can judge an author. If you are cautious and thorough in your approach, you can evaluate and critique an author's work as well as anyone. And once you have explored these thoughts, you will not only have a critic's insight into fiction, but you will enjoy it much more. See Table 8 for additional guidelines.

6. Develop Your Own Point of View.

After much research on the author's point of view, it's time to shift your focus. You should now know what the author thinks and what shaped his or her thinking. Knowing these things has helped you understand and appreciate the literary work. But there's more to think about.

How do you feel about the author's values, opinions, and beliefs? Do you agree with them? Are the morals and ethics consistent with yours? In what ways? In what ways are they different? What would you say to the author? In what ways have times changed that might make your point of view stronger than the author's? Once you have thought about these questions, present a clear and easy-to-follow thesis. State what the author says, what you think, and why your point of view is valid. Back up your thesis with well thought out arguments, and wrap it up with a succinct conclusion. Your critique will then represent a strong stand regarding the materials. It will have plenty of substance and be something you're proud to submit.

Table 8.
A Guide for Evaluating Literature

Literary Characteristic	Example	Description/ Evaluation	Remarks
Clarity of style	Works by Ernest Hemingway	Simple language, vivid description.	Classic style.
	Works by John Steinbeck	Clear language, depiction of real life experiences, believable and real characters.	Often depressing themes.
	Works by Ayn Rand	Logical thought, uses comparisons of people as they are to people as they should be.	Idealistic and often pollyanna endings.
	Works by Fyodor Dostoevsky	Well-defined true-to-life characters, straight-line type development of characters.	Characters almost become stereotyped.
Lack of Clarity	Works by James Joyce	Stream of consciousness style of writing, uses flashbacks, flash-fowards, element of unreality.	Story line is often bewildering and hard to follow. Relationships between events difficult to determine.
	Works by Edward Albee	Uses symbolism dealing with author's innermost feelings, as typified by the play, **Tiny Alice.**	Difficult to understand, hard to relate to author's experiences because of symbolic plot structure.
Realism	Works by Fyodor Dostoevsky	Complicated plots dealing with real people, true-to-life situations, and believable events, as typified by the novel **Crime and Punishment.**	

Table 8.
A Guide for Evaluating Literature *(continued)*

Literary Characteristic	Example	Description/ Evaluation	Remarks
Surrealism	Works by Anthony Burgess	Use of extremes and shock to develop satirical themes, as typified by the novel **A Clockwork Orange.**	Language is virtually a foreign language. Must understand author's purpose in order to understand plot and theme.
Escapism	Works by Ian Fleming	Use of mystery and suspense. Themes tend to avoid serious life problems. Characters are heroic, larger than life.	Typified by James Bond stories.
	Works by J.R.R. Tolkien	Use of fantasy. Reality is suspended.	Fables—almost an Alice in Wonderland quality.
Theme of morality	Contrast **War and Peace** by Tolstoy with **Barabas** by Lagkervist	Moral conflicts. Hero is faced with a decision of what is morally right	Often depressing yet important conflicts.
Political Themes	Contrast **The Memoirs of Richard Nixon** with books written by John Dean, H.L. Haldeman, and John Erlichman	Political writings.	Note how diiferent authors treat the same historical event.
Religious	Contrast **Angels** by Billy Graham with **The Faith of a Rationalist** by Bertrand Russell	Theological writings. Develop extensive background in both Eastern and Western theology.	Watch how each builds his case for or against theology.

Table 8.
A Guide for Evaluating Literature *(continued)*

Literary Characteristic	Example	Description/ Evaluation	Remarks
Themes of philosophy	Contrast **The Communist Manifesto** by Karl Marx with **Atlas Shrugged** by Ayn Rand	Contrast extremes.	Books with philosophical themes reflect opposites in the author's ideology.
Artistic Detail	Works by Tennessee Williams	Economy of words approaches poetry. Creation of character is based on creating empathy, as typified in the character of Blanche in the play **A Streetcar Named Desire**	Note usage of language, color and symbolism.
	Works by Thomas Wolfe	Use of nostalgic description, as typified by **Look Homeward Angel.**	

REVIEW THESE POINTS

How to Evaluate Fiction

1. Prepare for reading.
2. Meet the author.
3. Organize the information.
4. Ask questions before and after reading.
5. Learn ways to evaluate an author's work.
   - Examine the author's objective.
   - Analyze the characters.
   - Determine the author's writing style and mechanics.
   - Ascertain the author's viewpoint.
6. Develop your own point of view.

Figure 18.
Sample Notes* for Chapter 8

*See pages 103–107 for a description of how to prepare creative notes like these.

WRITE LIKE A WIZARD:

The Secret of Term Papers

"The most beautiful things in the world are the most useless."

> *Ruskin*

For most students, writing a long paper is a terror. Few things are dreaded more, and for good reason. No one is really taught how to research and write a paper, so most go about it inefficiently. Yet when done properly, a research paper can not only be written quickly, but can be a lot of fun. This chapter shows you, step-by-step, how to produce the best paper you are capable of writing. The method outlined will make any paper well structured and persuasive, and help you present your material for maximum results.

STEPS FOR WRITING RESEARCH PAPERS

1. Start with an Idea.

All research and term papers need a starting point. You'll either be assigned a topic or get to choose one on your own. In either case, you'll want to do some preliminary exploring. You can sort through your own textbook or notes to find a topic, or you can go to the library and do some exploratory research.

Pick a topic that appeals to you, one that you're interested in learning about. Once you've picked a possible topic, do a bit of follow-up to determine whether or not it's the right one for you.

To get general information about a topic, read an authoritative article on the subject, such as one in an encyclopedia. Does the topic still seem interesting to you? Can you tell if it's going to be too narrow or too broad? Does it have some controversy to it? Timeliness? A sufficient number of other sources? Only after you have answered these questions can you make an informed and accurate decision about your final topic.

2. Begin Shaping Your Topic.

After you have made your initial decision about the topic, you'll want to take it to the next level of development. Now you'll need a point of view for your paper. Think about a thesis, an argument, a direction for the topic. As an example, doing a paper on the growth of the civil rights movement in America would be a major undertaking. However, if you focused on the key role of President Lyndon Johnson or the role of the media, you'd have a narrower topic and a possible point of view.

The next step in shaping your ideas is to begin a rough outline. But include only main or key ideas in this preliminary outline. Start with your topic in the center and make branches coming out of it like the spokes of a wheel. Put different areas you want to talk about on different branches. Then you can visually see how many subtopics you have and how much information you can expect to generate for each of them. Soon you'll have an idea of how much you have to work with and what else you need to learn.

3. Gather Your Sources.

The best place to make your first run on information is the library. Look up your topic in the card catalog (or on the computer catalog, if your library has one). Check a general index to magazine articles such as *The Reader's Guide to Periodical Literature*, or appropriate specialized indexes such as the *Humanities Index* or *The New York Times Index*. Do an online bibliographic computer search for your topic, if your library has this service. Use other reference books, such as encyclopedias and bibliographic publications that are available for many subjects, to locate what might be important sources. Depending on your topic, you might find that the pamphlet or map sections have useful information for you. Of course, a great source for getting information about your subject is the reference librarian. Don't hesitate to ask for suggestions and direction at any point in your search. The librarian will also be able to give you basic general guidance about how to use the library.

The preliminary bibliography you prepare will serve you in many ways. First, it's great to find out early on in your project if you have adequate information for the research you need to do. Second, by collecting your sources early, you can process requests for interlibrary loans, if necessary. And lastly, the information you gather may further shape or refine your original title.

Be sure to use the most recent publications so

that your research provides the reader with the advantage of the most accurate and up-to-date information. Collect more sources than you think you'll need; many of the sources may not turn out to be as useful as you thought they would be. Plus, some of the sources may suggest others. List each source on a separate 3 × 5-inch index card. Include author, title, publisher, date and place of publication, edition, card catalog number, pages used, and your comments about the appropriateness of the source (e.g., core source, borderline source).

4. Gather Information from Your Sources.

Now you're ready to begin gathering pertinent data from your sources. Start with the easiest and most general sources first. Look for basic information on your topic, then scan it. Begin to build your subject knowledge, and start making a mental note of names and places that appear several times. Gain more and more background on the topic, moving from source to source.

Mark your source index cards with a notation to reference any especially key source. On the back of each 3 × 5-inch card, put any key ideas from the material. That way, you'll only need to look up a source once, unless it's one of the few that you decide to study in depth later. In general, try to spend only a few minutes on each source, before moving on to the next.

5. Map Out the Paper's Structure.

Now that you've narrowed the topic, located relevant sources, and gained background on the subject, you're ready to begin a structural formulation. This means you need to begin to see your paper's skeleton before you start adding the "flesh" of your writing. Your paper will have several predictable sections.

- **Introduction**
  Grab the reader's interest with an unusual story.
  Introduce the topic to the reader—its scope, width, and direction.
  State the importance, timeliness, and impact of the topic.
  Tell why you chose the topic.
  Summarize your thesis in a clear, concise statement.
  Motivate or tantalize the reader to read on.
- **Background**
  Give a brief history of the topic—be interesting.
  Briefly introduce other areas of your topic.
  Help the reader know what you know—key points only.
  Explain any terminology, key words, phrases.
- **Main Body**
  State strongly and truthfully your thesis and viewpoint.

Use accurate, strong, unemotional language.
Present arguments and ideas in easy-to-agree order:
from least to most controversial
from strongest to weakest in reasoning

- **Counter-Argument and Rebuttal**
State any opposing viewpoints.
Assess their strengths and weaknesses.
Build a case to further reinforce your thesis.
- **Conclusion**
Restate your thesis and your reasons for believing in it.
Briefly walk reader through your arguments and ideas.
Analyze and evaluate your key points for the reader.
Introduce no new information; restate prior ideas clearly.
Conclude with a succinct and moving statement.

6. Write the Rough Draft.

You have the first two key ingredients to begin writing: the background notes and the structural framework. How do you know how much to write on each section of the paper? One thing that may help you is to make some guesses about the final length you want your paper to be. Then start assigning approximate page lengths to each part.

- Introduction 5–12%
- Background 12–20%
- Body 40–60%
- Rebuttal 5–15%
- Conclusion 8–10%

For example, on a twenty-page paper, your introduction might be two pages, background three pages, body twelve pages, rebuttal two pages, and conclusion one page. This is only a guideline. Your teacher may have different standards. Check what the expectations are before you begin writing your rough draft.

For most people, the easiest way to write by far is to use a word processor. If you don't have one, many libraries and full-service copy shops can rent one to you. You may also have a friend who has one who can show you how to use it. The word processor is far superior to a typewriter or to writing by hand, it is well worth the time invested in learning how to use it.

Now is the time to start writing. But instead of starting at the beginning, start with the section on background. The introduction is much easier to write AFTER you have done most of the paper. Plus, the background gets you grounded and refamiliarized with the material. The material is easy to state, easy to organize, and easy to say a lot about.

After the background section is complete, move right on to the main body of the paper. Write for an hour at a time, then take a short break. As soon as you can, while you're fresh, go right back to it again. Keep the stream of thoughts coming, and write as long as you're producing good material. If you get stuck, take a longer break and come back when you're rejuvenated. There's no rule to follow about writing papers—just write as long as it's working. Some students can write well into the night and others do best in the morning, from about nine until noon. Just write when you're at your best and keep going until it's done. Then get away from it for a while.

7. Edit and Proofread.

After you have taken a break from your material, go back and read it aloud. It should read well, as if you were hearing a speech on your topic. Put in transition phrases where necessary. Make sure all the spelling is correct. Check for errors in logic and data. Double-check to insure you have avoided plagiarism. Make sure you have given credit where it is due. Have another set of eyes go over the paper, such as your friend's, so you get feedback. Add stronger words (use a thesaurus) to increase the clarity or impact. Consult a handbook on style and usage to insure that you have used the proper format for your paper and that your grammar is correct.

8. Prepare Paper for Presentation.

Documentation is the next to the last step. An excellent resource for this process is *10 Steps in*

Writing the Research Paper by Roberta and Peter Markham and Marie Waddell. Make sure you have given credit where it is due, that you have either inserted quotation marks or set off any quoted material, and that you have given correct and complete references for your sources.

The bibliography is always the last section of the paper. Use the bibliography cards you made when you began your research. The three most common types of entries you will need to know are:

1. **Books**

   Jensen, Eric. *You Can Succeed*. New York: Barron's Educational Series, 1989.

2. **Articles, Reports**

   Bills, R.E. "The Effect of a Value on Learn ing." *Journal of Personality* 21 (1952): 217- 22.

3. **Other sources**

   Olney, Claude. "Where There's a Will There's an A." Scottsdale, Arizona: Seminar Cassette Program, 1986.

Your final paper needs to be typewritten (or computer printed) on regular white bond paper. It should be done with black ink, double spaced, with 1½-inch margins on each side. Make sure that you number all the pages. Put your paper into a folder, and give it a title page. Center the title and put your name under it. Also include the date, name of course and instructor, and any special designations your class may have. Make sure your paper is perfect in its presentation: no smudges, stray marks, or errors. The neatness of your paper does affect the grading, whether it's a conscious decision by the instructor or not. Be meticulous and rigorous in assessing the quality of your paper before you turn it in (on time!). If you follow all of these steps carefully, you'll have a good shot at getting an *A*.

THE WRITING WILL NOW BE EASY!

"When you take good notes and organize them into a logical sequence, your term paper will practically write itself."

Table 9.
Organization of a Research Paper

PARTS	POINTS TO COVER
Introduction	Interest Grabber Introduction of Topic Explanation of Topic's Importance, Timeliness, and Impact Statement of Thesis Reader Motivation
Background	Historical Background of Topic Key Points About Topic Definitions of Key Words and Phrases
Main Body	Strong Statement of Thesis and Viewpoint Presentation of Contentions
Counter- Arguments and Rebuttal	Presentation of Other Viewpoints Discussion of Other's Strengths and Weaknesses Rebuttal
Conclusion	Restatement of Thesis to Persuade Review of Best Argument

REVIEW THESE POINTS

Steps for Writing Research Papers

1. Start with an idea.
2. Begin shaping your topic.
3. Gather your sources.
4. Gather information from your sources.
5. Map out the paper's structure.
6. Write the rough draft.
7. Edit and proofread.

CHAPTER 10

HOW TO TAKE TESTS:

Scoring What You're Worth

"The best students study what they don't know, not what they know."

Jensen

PREPARING FOR TESTING

The first and most obvious preparation for taking tests is to study beforehand. But an effective study procedure that will help ensure success is one that is planned from the beginning of the course and carried on, step-by-step, throughout the school term.

1. First Few Weeks of Classes.

To ace your tests, start the first week of school. Find out about your instructor. What is his or her favorite topic or author? Is student creativity encouraged or is the class run by the rules? What kind of class work is expected? Exactly what should your homework look like? Try to read ahead in your texts. Take notes before you go to class; it saves time and increases your understanding. As you read, ask yourself questions or bring them to class. Add class lecture notes to your home text notes, always trying to consolidate and unify them.

2. Middle of Course.

Try to study a little every day. It's a lot more effective and less stressful than cramming. Ask questions when you don't understand course material—don't put them off or you will forget about them. See your professor for extra help early in the term, not the day before a test. This will show a genuine interest on your part, and the extra contact will pay off at test time. Most important, be sure to introduce yourself, give your name twice, and make the most favorable impression you can. It's also helpful to ask your professor if he or she has any suggested reading material outside of assigned class texts. Even if you don't read that material, let your teacher know you're interested. The secret is to show some genuine interest in both your class subject and the professor. He or she is like anyone else and appreciates the personal touch.

Read as much background material as possible. The more you read about a topic, the greater your understanding, and the faster you will be able to read it. Gaining a wide background in a subject area will give you a big edge at test time. Another student may read the text and be able to recall most of it, but you will have the advantage even if you can recall only part of the additional reading you have done. You should also check your notes occasionally to make sure they are familiar and unstandable.

3. The Last Week Before the Test.

Find out what kind of exam will be given and alter your studying accordingly. If an objective test is scheduled, use memory techniques and concentrate on details. For a subjective or essay exam, the best approach is to get a wide background in that subject, stressing ideas rather than details. Concentrate on knowing something about almost everything. Rework your notes into a new format, trying to see the material from new angles. Review sessions are helpful, but get together with others only if they are good students. Otherwise, you will be really "soaked" for information, and learn nothing yourself. A *C* student usually doesn't enlighten an honor student, so study with the best students you can.

4. Last Few Days Before the Test.

At this point, start identifying what you don't know. Many students review by going over material they already know well. Often, parts they don't know are ignored, making their study process ineffective. Don't pat yourself on the back for what you do know, find out what you don't know. Remember this secret on how to study for tests: Turn to the index of your textbook and start with the first entry. Ask yourself if you understand that term, and continue until you come across an unfamiliar term. Look it up in the text, read about it, then take notes on it so you won't forget again. This system allows you to check yourself on every term, idea, person, and detail in the entire textbook. If your test is only on chapters seven and eight, just turn to the table of contents and find out which pages those chapters cover. Suppose those chapters include pages 77 through 102. Turn to the index again, and start at the beginning again. But this time look down the right side, noting only the terms that are on pages 77 through 102. That way you will study only the chapters you will be tested on.

Turn to the end of your text chapters and review a summary or listing of author's questions.

This can be helpful in directing your study efforts. At many colleges and universities, tests used during previous terms are kept on file in the library. These can be a gold mine because many professors don't rewrite a test each term. Often the tests used may just be scrambled questions from old tests. The prepared student has an easy *A*.

Many students find the use of homemade flash cards ideal, because they are portable and sometimes even fun. You might put a possible test question on one side and the answer on the other. Make notes on any data you seem to forget easily. Certain things seem very easy to remember and others seem easy to forget. But remember, if you forget it once, you will forget it again unless you write it down.

A positive attitude is crucial the few days prior to an exam. The upcoming test is not an execution; it is just a chance to show what you have learned. Your instructors want you to get good grades because it reflects on their teaching success. Most instructors feel bad when students do poorly because that mirrors their failure to communicate important concepts.

Look at the exam as a challenge and an opportunity to show what you have learned. Admit to yourself that you probably won't know every question; that way, you won't get discouraged when you see a test question you can't answer. Tests are necessary in most subjects. They're about the only way the professor knows you know the material.

5. Hours Before the Exam.

You have already run the hardest part of the race. If you have kept up during the term, you have already passed the exam; now it is the difference between an *A* and a *B*. Others may have exam fever, but you can relax a bit. Get a full night's sleep and be sure to get some exercise the day of the exam. That encourages better blood circulation, hence a better supply of oxygen to your brain during exam time. You will be able to think more clearly. It is best to exercise in moderation so that you are invigorated rather than exhausted. A brisk walk before the test is a good way to get exercise. Eat good foods, but eat lightly or not at all within an hour of your test. If you do eat, your body's energy and blood supply will be drawn toward your stomach for digestion instead of toward your brain where it is needed during test time.

Be sure to review all notes and texts. Browse through each chapter, making certain to expose your mind to as much information as possible. If you have kept up, all will be a review and cramming won't be necessary. Your confi-

PREPARATON MEANS *CONFIDENCE!*

"If you have kept up during the term, you have already passed the exam; now it is the difference between an *A* and a *B*."

dence and calm mental attitude will encourage recall at test time. A review on the night before the test should take only two to three hours. On the day of the exam arrive five to ten minutes early to your class. The best way to relax is to prepare mentally. Get the seat you want in class and practice recalling.

6. Exam Time.

Now you can cash in your efforts. First, read the entire exam thoroughly. By seeing questions in advance, you will give your subconscious mind time to come up with answers. Second, allot your time wisely. Note which questions are given the most point value and which are most difficult. Don't pick up your pen for a few minutes. Stop to think about your attack plan. Be relaxed and calm while you plan your approach. A good test taker doesn't fight tests; the secret is to relax.

Interpret and rephrase questions several ways to be sure you understand them. Then, start with the easiest problems first, and work quickly and neatly. Structure and organize before you answer because neatness does count, regardless of what an instructor will say. Be sure to keep in mind the test directions as you answer. Don't over read questions by assuming they are more complex than at first glance. Read them for what you believe is the intent of the question. Notice critical or key words in each question such as "show," "contrast," "define," and other similar directions.

Try to answer every question unless you absolutely have no idea of the answer; wrong answers are often subtracted from right ones.

TAKING OBJECTIVE TESTS

Objective tests are those that include questions in a true-false, multiple-choice, matching, or fill-in format. Usually the answer is provided but the student must decide among several possibilities.

1. True-false Questions.

True-false questions are the easiest test questions for the obvious reason that you have at least a fifty-fifty chance of getting the right answer. First, be sure you have read the question correctly. Look for words such as *always* or *never*, these words often indicate a false answer. Words such as *often, usually, rarely,* or *sometimes* can indicate a true answer. Decide if the statement is totally true before you mark it true. Answer what the tester intended, not what you read into the question. For example, the statement, "General Motors produces compact cars," is true. If the question had read, "General Motors *alone* produces compact cars," then it would be false. On true-false questions, stick with your first impression. Studies have shown over and over that your first impression is usually right, so be slow to change your answer, if at all. Remember, a statement is more likely to be true if it is a fairly long statement; it takes more qualifiers to make a true statement than a false one.

2. Multiple-choice Questions.

When answering multiple-choice questions, remember to read the answers first. This way, you'll view each answer separately and equally, without "jumping" on the first and easiest one. Look for an answer that not only seems right on its own, but completes the question smoothly. If the question asks why something occurs, then your answer must be a cause. Try to eliminate any obviously poor answers. Suspect as a possible right answer phrases such as "all of the above," "none of the above," or "two of the above." Check the wording of questions to notice qualifying phrases such as "all of the following are true *except* . . ." or "which two of the below are *not* . . ." Statistically, the least likely correct answer on a multiple-choice question is the first choice. When in doubt, pick the longer of the two answers. But, just as in true-false sections, always put something down. Even an educated guess is better than leaving the question blank and getting it wrong for sure.

3. Sentence Completion or Fill-in Questions.

These generally ask for an exact word from memory. They don't allow for much error, so make sure your answer is a logical part of the sentence as a whole. Use the length and number of blanks given as a hint. Make sure the grammar is consistent. When in doubt, guess. Even if it's a generalized guess, you may get partial credit. If you are unsure of two possibilities, include both and hope for half credit

TAKING ESSAY TESTS

When answering questions on an essay test, begin by making an outline on a piece of scratch paper. Assemble and organize the main points. Check the wording of the question to make sure you are interpreting it correctly. For example, if the question asks you to compare and contrast, do not give a description or a discussion. Begin your essay by using the same words that are in the question. Keep your answer to the point. Always write something in answer to a question, even if you don't have much to say.

Think and write by using this format.

1   Introduction—Introduce your topic.
2. Background—Give historical or philosophical background data to orient the reader to the topic.
3. Thesis and Arguments—State the main points, including causes and effects, methods used, dates, places, results.
4. Conclusion—Include the significance of each event and finish up with a summary.

When totally stumped for an answer on an essay, think about book titles, famous names, places, dates, wars, economics, and politics. Usually something will trigger some ideas. If you know nothing about the essay question, invent your own question on the subject and answer it. You'll usually get at least partial credit. That's better than nothing.

THE AFTERMATH

When you complete a test, be sure to reread all your answers. Check the wording of the questions again. Eliminate careless errors, and you can save a lot of disappointment later. This is the time when you can cash in on your brief encounters with your professor. Write your name in large, visible letters. If you have made a positive impression on your professor from personal contact, it will pay off now. Sometimes just a good impression can give you the higher grade in a borderline situation. Take as much time as you need When you think you have finished the test, turn it upside down on your desk. Think about it for a few minutes, giving your mind some time to relax and come up with some answers. If you still agree with what you have written, then turn it in. But sometimes those few moments spent just thinking about the questions will bring back the answer that gives the A.

Once your corrected test is returned, look it over. Check your errors and find out not what they were, but what kind of errors they were. Was it from answering questions too quickly, poor organization, a missed assignment, or incorrect notes? Understand why you made errors and avoid the problem on the next test.

REVIEW THESE POINTS

Preparing for Testing

1. First few weeks of classes.
   - Find out about your instructor.
   - Read ahead.
   - Take notes before class.
2. Middle of course.
   - Study every day.
   - Ask questions.
   - See your teacher.
   Read background material.
3. The last week before the test.
   - Find out about exam format.
   - Rework notes.
4. Last few days before the test.
   - Brush up on your weak areas.
   - Think positive.
5. Hours before the exam.
   - Sleep well.
   - Exercise.
   - Eat lightly.
   - Review your notes.
6. Exam time.
   - Read thoroughly.
   - Budget your time.
   - Interpret questions.

REVIEW THESE POINTS

Taking Objective Tests

1. True-false questions.
   - Look for key words.
   - Trust your first impression.
2. Multiple-choice questions.
   - Read answers first.
   - Eliminate poor choices.
   - Check wording of question.
3. Sentence completion or fill-in questions.
   - Make sure answer is logical.
   - Make sure grammar is consistent.
   - When in doubt, guess.

Taking Essay Tests

1. Outline.
2. Assemble and organize main points.
3. Write your introduction, background, thesis, and conclusion.

The Aftermath

1. Reread all answers.
2. Eliminate careless errors.
3. Take time to relax and rethink.
4. Afterwards, understand and learn from your errors.

Figure 19.
Sample Notes* for Chapter 10

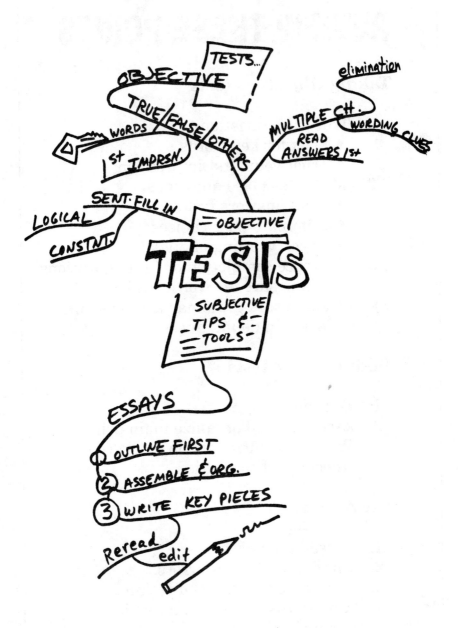

*See pages 103–107 for a description of how to prepare creative notes like these.

CHAPTER 11

THE SECRET

"The worst thing one can do is not to try, to be aware of what one wants and not give into it, to spend years in silent hurt wondering if something could have materialized—and never knowing."

David S. Viscott

Throughout the book I've talked about the importance of building successful habits. I've given you many ways to help yourself in school. As you've been able to tell, much of what is normally considered success in school can be achieved by positive thinking. In almost every chapter, you've seen how a positive approach can help you improve.

Yet, as vital as this is, there is more. Your mind is capable of much more, as it is your most powerful possession. Utilize what you've learned so far, then add the secret I'm about to give you and every problem can become an opportunity, every setback a shortcut, and every question an answer. The secret in this chapter will provide you with the last part of the formula for total success.

Like all real success formulas, the secret is simple. So far we have explored the conscious ways one can become successful. But perhaps you have never given thought to the other 88 percent of your mind, the subconscious.

One cannot overemphasize how fully it controls your life. Your subconscious mind functions automatically and ceaselessly twenty-four hours a day. It is an unlimited and perfect computer. It's a storehouse of forgotten dreams, nightmares, skills, and suggestions. And because it has the accumulations of a lifetime, much of its stored information is out of date. So, although your subconscious has the capacity of a $10 billion supercomputer, it is only as good as the programmer. Years ago, improper programming created bad habits that are not broken by the willpower of the conscious mind. To be a dynamic total success, *you must reprogram the subconscious mind.* Therein lies the secret!

PROGRAM YOURSELF FOR SUCCESS

The most direct and simple way to reprogram the subconscious mind is through relaxation and visualization. Under those conditions the door to your subconscious is wide open. Your master inner computer will accept suggestions easily and without question. You may have seen the power of suggestion demonstrated in a stage show. A timid, shy individual can be told that he is a great orator and he will proceed to give an eloquent talk to an amazed audience.

Every one of us passes through a brief hypnotic stage several times a day. This stage occurs just before falling asleep at night, upon awakening in the morning, and during times of extreme relaxation. During these moments of near sleep your normally argumentative conscious mind is not being used and suggestions are easily implanted in the subconscious mind. Why not use this natural state of mind to give positive suggestions of successful school habits directly to the subconscious, where they would be certain to take effect? After all, hypnosis merely implies a heightened state of suggestibility and there is nothing difficult or dangerous involved. It is totally safe and you are in full control at all times.

In self-programming, you'll discover a totally self-contained and self-controlled relaxed state of mind. You'll have full control over each suggestion. The suggestions you give yourself will go directly to your subconscious and allow you to reach your goals quickly and effortlessly. Not just any kind of suggestion will help, so let's define the proper kinds.

Suggestions, or affirmations as they are often called, have been used for thousands of years. An affirmation is a reinforcement tool used to affect our thoughts or actions in order to reach a goal. Affirmations can be written down, spoken, or visual. In order for affirmations to be effective, they should be positive, short, and in the present tense. For example, you would say, "I read rapidly and effortlessly," not, "I no longer read slowly."

You might ask, "How can I say I'm a fast reader when I'm not? Aren't I lying?" No, you are not lying. You are using your power of choice to reprogram your subconscious. After all, it does not know the difference between true or false. It will accept, without questioning anything you program into it. Therefore, if you repeatedly state "I *am* a rapid reader," you'll find your subconscious mind accepting that affirmation and soon you'll be one.

Affirmations can become doubly effective when coupled with another tool, visualizations. As you program your subconscious with each positive suggestion, visualize yourself having accomplished it. See yourself achieving that suggestion and reaching the goal you intended. Feel the excitement and joy of success. This will speed you on your way to realization of your goals.

You may already have a good idea of the goals you'd like to achieve while you're in school. If not, some of the more common ones are listed below with the corresponding affirmations you can use to help you reach those goals.

ELEVEN GOALS FOR YOU

GOAL 1: Improved Study Skills.

Suggested affirmations: I enjoy studying. I look forward to studying every day. I have plenty of time to study and find every subject interesting. I am enthusiastic and excited about studying. I always browse through textbooks before reading them. I observe the style, organization, and vocabulary. I prepare each section before reading. I gather main ideas quickly and easily. I read my texts with excellent comprehension. I review each chapter quickly and thoroughly. My notes are superb.

GOAL 2: Better Reading Skills.

Suggested affirmations: I love to read and find plenty of time for reading. I read quickly and effortlessly. I read in large word groups, absorbing difficult material without hesitation. My comprehension is perfect, as is my retention.

GOAL 3: Improved Notetaking.

Suggested affirmations: I enjoy taking notes and find them easy to do well. My notes represent the material clearly and creatively. I use my own shorthand and vary the size and shape of headings. I know the basic formats of most subjects and use them when designing my notes

GOAL 4: Improved Memory.

Suggested affirmations: My memory is perfect and I enjoy remembering information. I retain my material with ease and completeness. My memory is improving and I am more aware each day. Whatever information I need comes to me instantly and easily through perfect recall.

GOAL 5: Increasing Vocabulary.

Suggested affirmations: I have an ever increasing vocabulary and enjoy learning new words. I read new and unusual materials, thus adding new words daily. I have flash cards and practice them daily. I associate with those who have an excellent vocabulary to learn new words. I use the dictionary to increase my vocabulary. I notice how new words are spelled and check for the word roots. I enjoy an excellent vocabulary and use it daily.

GOAL 6: Better Test Taking.

Suggested affirmations: I look forward to taking tests and enjoy the opportunity to show what I know. I prepare myself thoroughly for each test. I review all class lecture notes, textbook notes, and related data. I easily memorize all pertinent information. I am confident and relaxed at exam time. I first preview the test, then plan my strategy. I move quickly and effortlessly through the exam. Correct answers come to mind instantly. My answers are clear and true. I am a successful test taker.

GOAL 7: Concentration.

Suggested affirmations: I am able to concentrate with ease. I block out distractions quickly and automatically. I focus my mind on the task at hand and complete it accurately. Other noises that I hear are normal everyday sounds, which flow with my thinking and increase my concentration.

GOAL 8: Better Health.

Suggested affirmations: I enjoy perfect health. I am energetic, enthusiastic, and outgoing. I enjoy small portions of health-giving wholesome foods. I experience an abundance of energy, vibrance, and youth. My body functions perfectly. I am alert, healthy, and strong. I keep my body in perfect condition and exercise daily. I enjoy exercising and my body is becoming firmer, stronger, and full of vitality. I think only thoughts of health, energy, and life.

GOAL 9: Liking School.

Suggested affirmations: I enjoy my classes and look forward to attending them daily. I thirst for knowledge. I satisfy my need for knowledge by attending all my classes and consulting my instructor. I find school challenging, rewarding, and positive. I meet interesting people at school and form satisfying relationships. I have an intense desire to become a success, and school is the key for me.

GOAL 10: Thinking Positively of Others.

Suggested affirmations: I enjoy positive thoughts. I look for the good in others. I practice the golden rule, knowing that a smile is powerful. I feel comfortable with others and find compliments easy to give. I allow others to be who they are, and give them understanding and warmth.

GOAL 11: Increased Confidence.

Suggested affirmations: I am the most important person in my world. I am successful. I am an intelligent free-willed being with the power to choose. I am talented, capable, and honest. I am warm, sincere, worthy, and creative. I like myself. I have a tremendous and unlimited potential. I love myself and appreciate my talents and abilities. I am unique and rare. I am valuable and rich in thought. I am an expression of love, happiness, and confidence. I believe in myself and my future. I am calm, relaxed, and confident in any situation. I control my destiny. I am free.

From the preceding suggestions, pick the affirmations that will help you reach the goals you desire. Many students find that writing affirmations down on 3 x 5-inch cards helps to clarify exactly what is wanted and is a convenient way to reinforce the goals. Anytime you have some free moments, you can read through your affirmations for reinforcement. By the way, there is no limit to the number of affirmations you may use.

Are you ready to put it all together? Let's first be aware that hypnosis is a perfectly natural state of mind. During the relaxed state that occurs between sleep and waking consciousness, you will feel peaceful, serene, and passive. You will hear normal outside noises but they will not disturb you. You will be able to think clearly but often your mind will wander.

Upon awakening from their first self-programming experience, students will often say, "I didn't feel a thing." They will often wonder if they were even in a trance. But each time self-programming is used, you'll find yourself going into relaxation more deeply and more quickly. Therefore, do not concern yourself with the degree of depth. The suggestions will reach your subconscious; repetition is the key.

There are many symptoms of a receptive state for self-programming, but initially do not concern yourself with the technical nature. Simply allow yourself to relax and you may experience several of the symptoms below indicating you are in a receptive state:

1. Physical relaxation.
2. Head and hands fall to side.
3. Heaviness of limbs.
4. Deep and rhythmic breathing.
5. Wanting to swallow.
6. Tingling sensation in fingers and toes.
7. Hand moves slowly to scratch an itch.
8. Sounds fade in and out.
9. Drowsiness and motionlessness.
10. Time passes quickly.

DIRECTIONS FOR SELF-PROGRAMMING

Here are ten simple steps for you to induce the state necessary for self-programming. There are other techniques, but this particular method is extremely easy, yet effective.

1. Collect your affirmations (self-improvement suggestions on 3 × 5-inch cards).
2. Relax in a comfortable chair.
3. Read your affirmations.
4. Close your eyes and relax.
5. Inhale deeply, hold your breath to the count of four, then exhale slowly.
6. Inhale deeply, hold your breath to the count of six, then exhale slowly.
7. Inhale deeply, hold your breath to the count of eight, then exhale slowly.
8. Starting with the muscles in your neck, relax each of your major muscles. Do your shoulders, arms, hands. Continue down as you relax your stomach, thighs, and legs. Relax every muscle in your body and allow it to remain loose and limp.
9. Visualize the accomplishment of your affirmations. Imagine your successes in great detail. See the goal attained and actually feel the excitement.
10. Slowly awaken yourself by counting from one to five. During this brief re-entry to your conscious mind, give yourself suggestions of happiness, alertness, and vitality.

You may choose to remain in a receptive state

for as little as five minutes or as long as thirty minutes. The length is not as important as the frequency. Use your self-programming often because the more often you gain access to your subconscious, the faster you'll reach your goals.

Practice at least once per day, although three times per day would be more helpful. Here are some good times to practice: Upon awakening in the morning, during a break, on a picnic in a park, while sunning yourself, during a boring TV show, and before you get out of your car.

Sometimes students become overwhelmed at this point because it all seems so complicated. But the procedure is incredibly simple and rewarding. You can change old bad habits without effort or sacrifice. Each time you read your affirmations something positive happens.

You are making a definite step towards your goal because every affirmation will register. Do not become discouraged if the results are not immediate. As long as you continue to use your self-programming, you are breaking down old objections and resistance. The positive suggestions will then become stronger than the old habits and you will begin acting successfully. It will be comfortable and natural.

You may be amazed to realize that you once objected to your new goals and now it seems so normal. You will have established a new habit pattern, improved your confidence, self-image, and, of course, your school habits. More important, you'll affirm and be forever aware that you are in control of your life. Your life will happen by your design and not by chance. Therefore, if you design it well, through effective affirmations, you can have the life you want.

Now that you have learned about affirmations, you can see the purpose of the Daily Scroll at the front of this book. In fact, you may want to include it in your daily self-programming. The use of the Daily Scroll can help make your progress even easier. Let's review the steps:

1. Decide on your goals.
2. Write down affirmations, which will help you reach your goals, on 3 × 5-inch cards.
3. Repeat your affirmations several times a day.

Simple enough, isn't it? Yes, it's a small price to pay for the benefits of being successful. Yet, this is the challenge for everyone, the challenge of change. Change is not easy sometimes, but in this case it *is* easy. And it's exciting. The feeling of success you'll acquire will be worth a lifetime of savings. There's nothing like it. For true success is not to be measured in the material world, it is a feeling. It's a gut-level feeling of pride, accomplishment, contentment, abundance, and joy. Because if you have that feeling, the feeling that self-programming and positive thinking can give to you, then you'll be a success in anything. Not just in school, but in relationships, athletics, business, and life.

AFFIRM YOUR GOALS!

"You'll affirm that you are in control of your life. Your life will happen by your design and not by chance . . . you can have the life you want."

CONCLUSION

My goal in this book was to give you three things. I wanted you *to realize* that you *can* become a total success in school. You have all the ability and talent in the world. Whatever you wish in life can be yours if you'll only realize it and accept it.

Secondly, I wanted to *motivate* you to achieve what you know you can. Everyone is motivated by different things and I hope you've found the right motivation for you to begin being successful. Reading this book shows you've already motivated yourself well.

Lastly, I wanted to give you the *tools* to achieve all the success that is rightfully yours. You've been given many valuable tools in this book: the knowledge of an excellent study procedure; how to read better, take more effective notes, improve your vocabulary, and improve your memory; techniques for evaluating fiction; how to write papers; and secrets to taking tests. You've learned how to program a better future through self-programming—and what an important tool that is! Now that you've finished this book, put what you've learned to use. You know you deserve success, so go for it!

BIBLIOGRAPHY

Armstrong, William. *Study in Hard Work.* New York: Harper & Row, 1967.

Bamman, Henry, and Lawrence Brammer. *How to Study Successfully.* Palo Alto, California: Pacific Books, 1969.

Belliston, Larry and Craig Mayfield. *Speed Learning.* Woodland Hills, California: SB Press, 1983.

Botkin, James. *No Limits to Learning.* Elmsford, New York: Pergamon Books, 1979.

Branden, Nathaniel. *The Psychology of Self-Esteem.* New York: Bantam, 1969.

Buzan, Tony. *Make the Most of Your Mind.* New York: Linden Press, 1984.

————. *Use Both Sides of Your Brain.* New York: Dutton, 1974.

Bromberg, Murray, and Melvin Gordon. *1100 Words You Need to Know.* 2nd ed. New York: Barron's Educational Series, Inc., 1987.

Bromberg, Murray, and Julius Liebb. *Hot Words for the SAT: The 350 Words You Need to Know.* New York: Barron's Educational Series, Inc., 1989.

Brown, James. *Efficient Reading.* Lexington: D.C. Heath & Co., 1967.

Campbell, David. *If You Don't Know Where You're Going, You'll Probably End Up Somewhere Else.* Niles, Illinois: Argus Communications, 1974.

Chapman, Elwood. *So You're a College Freshman*. Chicago: Science Research Associates, 1967.

Dudley, Geoffrey. *Increase Your Learning Power*. Hollywood: Wilshire, 1975.

Dunn-Rankin, Peter. "Visual Characteristics of Words." *Scientific American* 238:128, 1978.

Dyer, Wayne. *What Do You Really Want for Your Children?* New York: William Morrow & Co., 1985.

Fralick, Marsha. *Decisions Make It Happen*. La Mesa, California: Grossmont Union High Press, 1977.

Froe, Otis. *How to Become a Successful Student*. New York: Arco Publishing Co., 1959.

Garfield, Pat. *Creative Dreaming*. New York: Ballantine, 1974.

Gawain, Shakti. *Creative Visualization*. Berkeley, California: Whatever Publishing, 1979.

Glasser, William. *Schools Without Failure*. New York: Harper & Row, 1969.

Harrison, Allan. *How To Teach Children Twice As Much*. New York: Arlington House, 1973.

Hart, Leslie. *Human Brain and Human Learning*. New York: Longman, 1983.

Hill, Napoleon. *Think and Grow Rich*. New York: Fawcett, 1937.

Hutchison, Michael. *Megabrain*. New York: William Morrow & Co., 1986.

Jensen, Eric. *SuperTeaching*. San Diego: Turning Point, 1988.

———. *Impact Teaching*. San Diego: Turning Point, 1989.

Kranyik, Robert. *How to Teach Study Skills* New Jersey: Teachers Practical Press, 1963.

Laird, Donald and Eleanor. *Techniques for Efficient Remembering.* New York: McGraw-Hill, 1968.

Lakein, Alan. *How To Get Control Of Your Time and Your Life.* New York: Signet, 1974.

Lewis, Norman. *How to Read Better and Faster.* New York: John Wiley & Sons, 1969.

Lindgren, H. *The Psychology of College Success.* New York: John Wiley & Sons, 1969.

Lucas, Jerry, and Harry Lorayne. *The Memory Book.* New York: Macmillan, Inc., 1974.

MacDonald, Will, and Richard Bandler. *Insider's Guide to Submodalities.* Cupertino, California: Meta Publications, 1988.

Maltz, Maxwell. *Psycho-Cybernetics.* Hollywood: Wilshire Book Co., 1960.

Mandino, Og. *The Greatest Miracle in the World.* New York: Bantam, 1975.

———. *The Greatest Salesman in the World.* New York: Bantam, 1968.

Markman, Roberta H., Peter T. Markman, and Marie L. Waddell. *Ten Steps in Writing the Research Paper.* 4th ed. New York: Barron's Educational Series, Inc., 1989.

Mayer, Dennis. *X-Rated Guide to Learning.* Fullerton, California: CPGA, 1978.

Millman, Jason. *How to Take Tests.* New York: McGraw-Hill, 1969.

Morgan, Clifford. *How to Study.* New York: McGraw-Hill, 1969.

Ornstein, Robert. *Psychology of Consciousness.* San Francisco: Penguin, 1974.

————. *The Mind Field.* New York: Pocket Books, 1976.

————. *The Amazing Brain.* Boston: Houghton-Mifflin Co., 1984.

Ostrander, Sheila, and Lynn Shroeder. *Super-Learning.* New York: Delta Press, 1979.

Rose, Colin. *Accelerated Learning.* London: Topaz Publishing, 1985.

Ross, John. "Resources of Binocular Perception." *Scientific American* (March 1976): 80.

Rusk, Thomas. *Treat Your Ego in 4 Hours.* New York: Peter Wyden Publisher, 1974.

Sill, Sterling. *How You Can Personally Profit from the Laws of Success.* Salt Lake City, Utah, NIFP (National Institute of Financial Planning), 1978.

Smith, Samuel. *Best Methods of Study.* New York: Barnes & Noble, 1968.

Strunk, William Jr., and E.B. White. *Elements of Style.* New York: Macmillan, Inc., 1979.

Youngs, Bettie. *Stress in Children.* New York: Arbor House, 1985.